LE PETIT
Labeaume
ILLUSTRÉ

JEAN-SIMON **GAGNÉ**
ANDRÉ-PHILIPPE **CÔTÉ**

LE PETIT **Labeaume** ILLUSTRÉ

LES ÉDITIONS
LA PRESSE

Catalogage avant publication de Bibliothèque et Archives nationales du Québec et Bibliothèque et Archives Canada
Gagné, Jean-Simon
Le petit Labeaume illustré
ISBN 978-2-923681-72-6

1. Labeaume, Régis, 1956- - Humour. 2. Labeaume, Régis, 1956- - Caricatures et dessins humoristiques. 3. Labeaume, Régis, 1956- - Citations. I. Côté, André-Philippe. II. Labeaume, Régis, 1956- . III. Titre.

FC2946.26.L32G33 2011
971.4'4710509 C2011-940681-0

DIRECTRICE DE L'ÉDITION
Martine Pelletier
TEXTES
Jean-Simon Gagné
CARICATURES
André-Philippe Côté
DESIGN ET INFOGRAPHIE
Yanick Nolet

L'éditeur bénéficie du soutien de la Société de développement des entreprises culturelles du Québec (SODEC) pour son programme d'édition et pour ses activités de promotion. L'éditeur remercie le gouvernement du Québec de l'aide financière accordée à l'édition de cet ouvrage par l'entremise du Programme de crédit d'impôt pour l'édition de livres, administré par la SODEC.

L'édtieur reconnaît l'aide financière du gouvernement du Canada par l'entremise du Programme d'aide au développement de l'industrie.

Dépôt légal – 1er trimestre 2011
ISBN 978-2-923681-72-6
Imprimé et relié au Canada

LES ÉDITIONS LA PRESSE

PRÉSIDENT
André Provencher
LES ÉDITIONS LA PRESSE
7, rue Saint-Jacques
Montréal (Québec) H2Y 1K9
514 285-4428

POUR L'AMOUR DU CIEL… RELAXE RÉGIS !

LABEAUME NE S'EST PAS BÂTI EN UN JOUR !

BEN VOYONS... AVANT LONGTEMPS, LES GENS PRENDRONT LE TGV JUSQU'À QUÉBEC ET ENSUITE LE TRAMWAY JUSQU'AU NOUVEL AMPHITHÉÂTRE POUR VOIR UN MATCH DES NORDIQUES !
800 MG DE LITHIUM 3 FOIS PAR JOUR !

L'époque pré-hystérique

QUÉBEC AVANT RÉGIS LABEAUME

Il était une fois un mirage. Non, attendez, ce n'est pas ça du tout. Il y a une faute de frappe. Allez, on recommence.

Il était une fois un virage. En 2005, Andrée Boucher a été élue triomphalement à la mairie de Québec. « La Reine maire », comme on l'appelait, ne voulait pas mettre un sou dans une candidature de Québec au Jeux olympiques d'hiver, rebaptisés les Olympiques-assiette. Madame se prononçait contre la construction d'un nouvel amphithéâtre, contre le retour des Nordiques, contre la construction d'un tramway, contre les voyages à l'étranger, contre la construction d'un anneau de glace intérieur, contre l'aménagement trop élaboré des berges du fleuve, et probablement contre les éco-quartiers derrière lesquels elle aurait vu une conspiration écolo-bolchévique. Pour la mairesse, il était hors de question que la Ville de Québec assume toute seule les risques du sauvetage du jardin zoologique ou même de la tenue d'un championnat mondial de hockey.

Jusqu'à son décès, le 24 août 2007, Andrée Boucher continuait à bénéficier d'un taux d'approbation fort respectable de 65 %. À peine moins que ce qu'elle récoltait au faîte de sa gloire, à la mairie de Sainte-Foy. Comme elle répétait en substance : « J'aime mon public et mon public m'aime ».

Mais tout cela appartient à un passé révolu, pour ne pas dire à l'époque pré-hystérique. Aujourd'hui, un ange est passé. En 2011, le maire Régis Labeaume est pour la candidature de la ville aux Jeux olympiques d'hiver, pour la construction d'un nouvel amphithéâtre, pour le retour des Nordiques, pour le tramway, pour la construction d'un anneau de glace intérieur, pour les voyages à l'étranger, pour l'aménagement des berges du fleuve et pour le développement d'éco-quartiers.

Les derniers sondages le créditent d'un taux d'approbation de plus de 80 %.

À quel moment s'est produit le déclic, la métamorphose, le virage à 180 degrés ? À quel moment l'opinion publique de Québec s'est-elle retournée comme un gant ?

Suggérons une date qui en vaut bien une autre.

Le 1er avril 2008, le jour du Poisson d'avril, le maire Régis Labeaume avait une grande nouvelle à annoncer sur les ondes de Radio-Canada. Le projet de complexe théâtral si cher à Robert Lepage, dans une cavité située sous la falaise, en plein centre-ville, était abandonné. En lieu et place, l'immense caverne servirait à l'installation d'une fondeuse à neige, générant une chute d'eau tiède, le long de la falaise. Pour calmer les opposants, M. Labeaume précisait même que l'eau de la chute ne serait pas fluorée!

Il s'agissait bien sûr d'un poisson d'avril, auquel le maire avait accepté de participer. Mais plusieurs auditeurs ont mordu à l'hameçon. Au point d'expédier des courriels rageurs pour dénoncer le projet.

Difficile à croire, mais un petit nombre de gens ont aussi tenu à signaler à Radio-Canada qu'ils appuyaient le projet du maire. À croire que M. Labeaume pouvait désormais leur faire avaler n'importe quoi.

Une nouvelle ère commençait...

PREMIER ACTE

LA FABRICATION D'UN MAIRE

STYLE L'ALLIER
STYLE LABEAUME

Résumé d'un téléfilm en quatre épisodes

Épisode 1 : La traversée du désert

Le 2 décembre 2007, Régis Labeaume remporte le premier prix d'un concours de circonstances, en devenant le maire de Québec.

Stop. N'allons pas trop vite. Après avoir aguiché le spectateur, comme dans tout téléfilm qui se respecte, ramenons-le quelques années en arrière. À l'époque où le héros connaît des débuts politiques difficiles.

En 1998, le millionnaire Régis Labeaume veut devenir candidat du Parti québécois dans la circonscription de Montmorency. Mais son numéro de « l'homme d'affaires qui a réussi » ne passe pas la rampe. Pas encore. Un autre candidat le devance par 80 votes.

En mars 2005, il tente de succéder au maire Jean-Paul L'Allier, à la tête du Renouveau municipal de Québec (RMQ). Malgré une campagne prometteuse, il termine au second rang, derrière Claude Larose, un politicien expérimenté mais qui possède autant de charisme qu'un grille-pain durant une panne d'électricité. Une claque, une vraie.

Chaque fois, Régis Labeaume croit que le destin frappe à la porte. Il enfile son costume du dimanche, il prépare les confettis et il sable le champagne. Il ouvre la porte, il se prépare à embrasser le destin et puis zut !, c'est encore un colporteur qui veut lui vendre un aspirateur...

Épisode 2 : L'heure la plus noire, c'est celle qui précède l'aurore

La carrière politique de Régis Labeaume ne décolle pas. La vie continue, mais le soir, quand tout le monde est couché, le héros regarde tristement l'horizon, en se répétant les mots de son idole, Winston Churchill. « Le succès consiste à naviguer de défaite en défaite sans jamais perdre son enthousiasme. »

Le pire est encore à venir.

Le 6 novembre 2005, l'ancienne mairesse de Sainte-Foy, Andrée Boucher, est élue à la mairie de Québec. Madame est fière d'avoir remporté la victoire sans pancarte, sans équipe et surtout sans programme. Elle se targue d'avoir dépensé 5 000 $. Autant dire une poignée de cacahouètes.

La nouvelle mairesse éprouve envers Régis Labeaume une antipathie toute particulière. Le vieux monarque sait toujours reconnaître un rival trop ambitieux, même si ce dernier est resté dans les coulisses. « Les millionnaires qui se cherchent des distractions, on n'a pas besoin de ça en politique municipale », persifle-t-elle à son endroit. Ouille ! Quand Madame la mairesse attaque, c'est pour envoyer l'adversaire au tapis.

Régis Labeaume, un millionnaire « en quête de distractions » ? L'expression aurait pu lui coller à la peau. Ruiner sa carrière.

Il n'en sera rien. Car l'improbable survient.

Le 24 août 2007, la mairesse Andrée Boucher meurt subitement. À Québec, la commotion est immense. À court de superlatifs et de larmes de crocodile, des journalistes surexcités comparent même la défunte à René Lévesque! Le culte de la mairesse devient un passage obligé pour tous les candidats. C'est à qui réussira à se draper tout entier dans le linceul de la défunte.

Pour Régis Labeaume, est-ce le crépuscule ou l'aurore? La fin du début?

L'épisode se termine sur un roulement de tambour, pour accompagner le héros qui va jouer le tout pour le tout.

Épisode 3 : Quitte ou double

La campagne de Régis Labeaume à la mairie commence mal.

Le premier sondage place l'ancien animateur de radio André Arthur au second rang des intentions de vote. Le futur maire n'arrive qu'en cinquième place, avec un microscopique 6 % des votes. Pas beaucoup plus que la proportion d'électeurs qui croient avoir été enlevés par des extraterrestres ou par le fantôme de la mairesse Boucher.

Mais Régis Labeaume va jouer deux coups de maître.

À la mi-novembre, à deux semaines du vote, il obtient l'appui de Marc Boucher, l'époux de la défunte mairesse. Un exploit, pour ne pas dire un miracle. Comme l'écrivait Yan Turgeon, dans le journal *Voir*, l'appui de Marc Boucher, équivalait alors « à un édit papal dans le Québec des années 50 ». [(1)]

(1) Yan Turgeon, « Marc Boucher, personnalité de Québec 2007 », *Voir*, 20 décembre 2007.

L'autre coup fumant de Régis Labeaume, c'est de s'assurer la complicité de deux importantes stations radiophoniques privées de Québec, CHOI-radio X et CJMF 93,3. En 2007, les deux stations exercent une influence considérable. Selon une recherche du Centre d'études sur les médias de l'Université Laval, les radios vont endosser la candidature de Régis Labeaume.(2) À l'opposé, elles vont dénigrer systématiquement la candidate du Renouveau municipal de Québec, Ann Bourget, qui semblait voguer vers une victoire facile. Dans la plus pure tradition radiophonique de Québec, des animateurs vont railler Mme Bourget parce qu'elle ne possède pas de voiture. Ou parce qu'elle n'a pas d'enfants.

Même la publicité du candidat Labeaume multiplie les clins d'oeil à la radio. « Régis Labeaume, mon CHOI X », peut-on lire sur l'une des pancartes du candidat.

(2) Colette Brin, Thierry Giasson et Dominique Payette, sous la direction de Florian Sauvageau et de Daniel Giroux, *Radio parlée, élections et démocratie*, Cahiers-Médias no 18, Centre d'études sur les médias, Université Laval, septembre 2009.

Épisode 4 : « Je suis venu, j'ai vu, j'ai vaincu »

Le 2 décembre 2007, Régis Labeaume remporte une éclatante victoire, en récoltant 60 % des suffrages.

Parti de nulle part, le nouveau maire a multiplié ses appuis par dix en l'espace de trois mois...

« Ils étaient orphelins [de la mairesse]. Ils m'ont adopté », confiera-t-il au *Devoir.* (3)

Mais le nouveau maire n'a pas encore trouvé ses marques. Au début, il n'est pas rare de l'entendre dire qu'il va faire « comme la mairesse ». Et il prend garde de ne jamais déplaire à ses alliés de la radio. Un animateur annonce triomphalement que son ami Régis va « botter des culs » à l'hôtel de ville de Québec. Un autre veut organiser une manifestation pour l'appuyer dans ses négociations avec les fonctionnaires...

Il faudra encore du temps pour que Régis Labeaume apprivoise son propre personnage. Un personnage que les fêtes du 400e anniversaire de la ville vont propulser sur la scène nationale, comme aucun autre maire de Québec avant lui.

« Je me suis fabriqué moi-même », pourra dire Régis Labeaume.

En attendant qu'un petit malin lui réponde : « Ah, c'est donc ça ! De toute évidence, vous n'aviez pas de manuel d'instructions... »

(3) Isabelle Porter, « Du phénomène Boucher au phénomène Labeaume », *Le Devoir*, 21 août 2008, p. a1.

LABEAUME CONTRE BOURGET

QUI M'AIME ME SUIVE !
RED BULL

Les Labeaumeries I

LES GRANDES CITATIONS DU MAIRE LABEAUME

« J'ai de la misère un petit peu. Le gars est énergique, mais je trouve qu'il est parfois épars. Il part sur des chires. (...) Je trouve que ça manque de cohérence. »

– À propos de Nicolas Sarkozy, à l'émission Bazzo.tv. à Télé-Québec, 9 octobre 2008.

« Je ne suis pas capable d'accepter que les syndiqués fourrent le système. »

-Entrevue à CHOI-FM, le 17 avril 2008.

« C'est son droit d'aînesse, n'oubliez que les maires passent, mais Bonhomme reste. (...) Si vous me demandez pourquoi Bonhomme est passé avant le maire, il n'y a rien de plus normal. »

– Essayant d'expliquer pourquoi le premier ministre du Canada, Stephen Harper, avait reçu le Bonhomme Carnaval avant lui, malgré ses demandes d'entretien répétées. *Le Soleil*, 27 novembre 2011.

« Si vous pensez que, actuellement, il y a du monde qui se préoccupe beaucoup d'une consultation [sur l'amphithéâtre], vous êtes en dehors de la planète. Ça n'existe pas actuellement. Le monde est rendu ailleurs. Ils se demandent quel club va venir à Québec. C'est ça, la vérité. »

– À propos d'une consultation publique sur l'amphithéâtre. *Le Soleil*, 7 mars 2011.

« Nous, on a hérité de ruines. »

– À propos de l'état des infrastructures de la ville de Québec. *Le Soleil*, 16 décembre 2010.

« La francophonie m'inquiète. Elle somnole, elle est inerte. »

– *Le Soleil*, 4 mars 2008.

« On a fait de l'amnésie. On ne s'en souvient pas. On n'en a pas parlé. »

– Un mois après ses déclations controversées, lors de sa rencontre à Paris avec le numéro Un de la Francophonie, Abdou Diouf, 7 avril 2008.

« Si vous êtes venus ici pour chialer, c'est pas la place ! »

– À son arrivée à une consultation publique sur la ville idéale, au Cégep de Sainte-Foy. 28 septembre 2010.

« Ça n'a pas une crisse de cenne et ça ne sait pas où en trouver non plus. »

– Commentaire sur les défenseurs du patrimoine « qui veulent tout conserver ». *Le Devoir*, 10 juillet 2009.

« Je m'entends bien avec Madame [Josée] Verner, mais y'a des fois où je la battrais. »

– À l'émission Bazzo.tv, à Télé-Québec, 9 octobre 2008.

« On pense qu'on va faire venir du monde de la Nouvelle-Zélande à Québec. Il n'y en aura pas de monde de Tombouctou. Il faut faire venir le gars de Brossard. »

– Sur le changement de cap du 400e. *Le Soleil*, 7 janvier 2008.

« *If you have a problem, call me.* »
[« Si t'as un problème, téléphone-moi ».]

– Au boxeur Bernard Hopkins, à la veille de son combat de championnat contre Jean Pascal, au Colisée Pepsi. *La Presse*, 16 décembre 2010.

« Ce ne sont pas ses idées qui sont minables, mais le gars lui-même. »

– Après une prise de bec avec un militant pacifiste, lors d'une cérémonie à la mémoire de soldats de Valcartier. *Le Soleil*, 14 juin 2008.

« Je pète une coche régulièrement. Et si je n'ai pas de raisons de le faire, j'en trouve une. »

– Entrevue au *Journal de Québec*, 2 octobre 2009.

« C'est pas le marketing sur le 400e qui a amené le monde à Québec cet été – il était tellement mauvais – c'est le produit. »

– À propos du travail de l'Office du tourisme, *Le Soleil*, 9 septembre 2008.

«Quand [bien] même on vous ferait un document de 20 pages, vous ne le liriez pas. La population ne les lit pas. (...) Vous allez accumuler les communiqués de presse et ça va être ça, la plate-forme.»

– À des journalistes qui s'étonnaient que sa plate-forme électorale tienne sur une seule page. *Le Soleil*, 25 septembre, 2009.

«Isabelle Porter [correspondante du *Devoir*] comment ça va? On est beaucoup à se demander pourquoi vous couvrez la ville encore? Bel exercice d'automutilation dans son article de la semaine passée. Beau journalisme de colonisé. Prochaine question.»

– En conférence de presse. 28 mars 2010.

«Le [Complexe) G n'est pas beau. La seule façon de régler notre problème, c'est de le faire oublier, et la seule façon de le faire oublier, c'est d'en avoir trois ou quatre autour, qui sont vraiment distinctifs, qui font en sorte qu'on ne voit plus le G.»

– Entrevue au journal *Le Soleil*. 4 juillet 2009.

«Salut la calotte. Tu votes pour moi? C'est-tu à cause de mon corps?»

– À un cégépien, durant la campagne électorale. *Le Soleil*, 30 octobre 2009.

MIROIR, MIROIR... MOI, SARKO, SUIS-JE TOUJOURS LE PLUS GRAND DES PETITS ?
EUH... NON, IL Y A UN PETIT MAIRE DANS LA VILLE DE QUÉBEC QUI POURRAIT VOUS DÉPASSER !

Journal imaginaire de Nicolas Sarkozy

AU TEMPS DU 12e SOMMET DE LA FRANCOPHONIE

Paris, le 12 octobre 2008

Ce matin, mon aide de camp m'a rapporté les propos du maire de Québec, Régis Labeaume, à mon sujet. Ça se passait à la télévision québécoise, il y a quelques jours.

Monsieur me trouve «énergique», mais «épars». Il trouve que je manque de «cohérence». Il affirme aussi que je partirals sur des... Sur des comment déjà ? Ah oui, sur des «chires». «Je pars sur des chires», à ce qu'il paraît.

Au début, je n'étais pas sûr d'avoir compris. Surtout le mot «chires». Franchement, je pensais qu'il s'agissait d'un problème gastro-intestinal. Il a fallu que mon aide de camp traduise... Non mais pour qui il se prend, ce mec? Pour le dernier spécimen de l'humour québécois, cette sous-culture du rire gras qui encombre nos salles de spectacle de troisième ordre ?

En plus, le malotru s'est permis de petites blagues sur Carla.

Pour me calmer, mon aide de camp m'a rapporté une histoire racontée par le comédien Claude Brasseur.

Un jour, que Brasseur jouait sur scène, un téléphone portable a sonné dans la salle. Alors Brasseur s'est approché du public, et il a dit : «Si c'est pour moi, dites que je travaille». Ha-ha-ha-ha. Ça, au moins, c'est pas de l'humour de mangeur de poutine...

Québec, le 17 octobre 2008

Enfin arrivé à Québec. Ici, le symbole de ce qu'ils appellent une capitale, c'est un gros hôtel en forme de gâteau à la crème. Le Château Frontispice ? Ou le Château Montignac ? Enfin, peu importe.

J'ai fini par rencontrer le maire Labeaume. Il a essayé de me faire le coup du vieux copain. Nous avons parlé d'affaires, de tourisme, ou peut-être de sa collection de tracteurs, je ne me souviens plus très bien.

Au moins, il n'est pas de grande taille. Ça m'a évité de porter mes bottillons à talons ultra-hauts, pour une fois.

À un certain moment, je l'observais à la dérobade. Comment des gens sains d'esprit ont-ils pu trouver la moindre ressemblance entre cet étrange personnage et moi ?

En après-midi, on a donné le coup d'envoi d'une espèce de surboum de pays plus ou moins francophones. Ils osent appeler cela le Sommet de la francophonie. Même la Bulgarie est invitée, ça vous donne une idée...

La présidence de la République, ça serait le pied s'il n'y avait pas toutes ces activités protocolaires assommantes. La vocation universelle de la France, je veux bien. Mais faut-il se taper le vice-président d'un canton suisse qui parle de sa recette de fondue? Ou le bourgmestre d'un obscur district du Laos, qui récite Lamartine? Pour me calmer, mon aide de camp m'a rappelé une citation de François Cavanna. Je crois bien que je vais en faire ma devise.

« Les cons ne mènent pas le monde, mais pour mener le monde, il faut plaire aux cons. »

Anacoluthes, amphitryons, autocrates,
bougres d'extrait de cornichon,
cachalots, cannibales emplumés,
coloquintes, clysopompes, hydrocarbures,
emplâtrés à la graisse de hérisson,
logarithmes, macrocéphales,
moules à gaufres...

Québec, le 18 octobre 2008

Le maire Labeaume et les autres voulaient à tout prix que j'aille inaugurer le cadeau que notre grande République a offert à la petite ville de Québec, pour son 400ᵉ anniversaire. Au début, je ne savais pas de quoi il s'agissait. Je m'attendais à un Arc de triomphe, ou à quelque chose qui respire la grandeur. À la rigueur, j'aurais donné ma bénédiction à une œuvre qui sème la controverse. Comme l'infâme cube blanc que Chirac a fait installer en plein milieu de leur Place Royale. Ha-ha-ha-ha ! Sacré Chirac ! Aussi approprié que de flanquer une cuillerée de moutarde dans un verre de bordeaux centenaire.

Quand on m'a dit que j'allais imaugurer le nouveau hall d'entrée d'un musée, dans le Vieux-Québec, j'ai failli défaillir. J'avais juste envie de les envoyer, comment ils disent, déjà ? Chirer ?

Pour me calmer, au moment de prendre l'avion pour Washington, mon aide de camp m'a rappelé ce que disait Serge Gainsbourg à propos de la chanson française : « Je suis plutôt consterné que concerné ».

Washington, le 19 octobre 2008

Au début, je voulais écrire ce journal en employant le « nous ». Jusqu'à ce que je tombe sur la citation d'un écrivain amerloque, Mark Twain, qui disait que le « nous » devrait être réservé « aux rois, aux présidents, aux éditeurs et aux gens qui sont infectés par le ver solitaire ». Alors j'ai changé d'idée.

Rendu à Washington, je croyais avoir enfin échappé à ces Québécois et à leur francophonie à la noix. Mais à peine arrivé, on me signale que mon discours devant l'Assemblée nationale de Québec a fait des vagues. Ils sont fous ces Québécois.

Dire que j'avais peur de ne pas en avoir mis assez. Dire que je croyais leur avoir servi une dose de platitudes capables d'engourdir tout un troupeau d'éléphants. Attendez que je me souvienne. « Le monde n'a pas besoin d'une autre division, ai-je dit. Les Canadiens sont nos amis. Les Québécois sont notre famille. » À un moment donné, je me suis même surpris à dire que je suivais « de très près » l'actualité politique du Québec et du Canada !

De « très près ». Ha-ha-ha-ha ! Elle est bien bonne ! Je m'en tape encore sur les cuisses ! Je n'allais quand même pas avouer que je m'intéresse davantage aux résultats de la seconde division de football qu'à l'actualité de cet immense champ de pergélisol qu'ils prennent pour un pays !

Pour me calmer, mon aide de camp m'a rappelé ce que j'avais déclaré à l'*Express*, en 1995 : « Avoir des ennemis, c'est la preuve que l'on existe ! »

Mais je crois bien que je vais m'endormir en me répétant une citation d'Oscar Wilde, bien plus douce à mon oreille présidentielle : « S'aimer soi-même, c'est l'assurance d'une longue histoire d'amour ».

LA FRANCE AIMERAIT CHANGER LA FORMULE DE " NON-INGÉRENCE ET NON-INDIFFÉRENCE " À L'ÉGARD DU QUÉBEC !

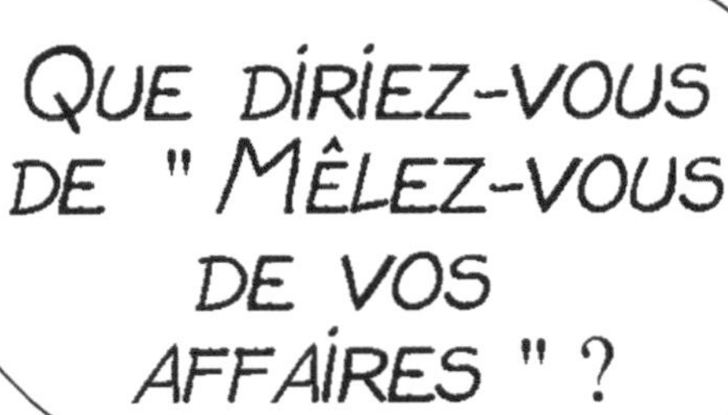
QUE DIRIEZ-VOUS DE "MÊLEZ-VOUS DE VOS AFFAIRES" ?

LE LABEAUME RÊVEUR

LE LABEAUME COLÉRIQUE

LE LABEAUME BOUDEUR

LE LABEAUME MOQUEUR...

Blanche-Québec et les sept Labeaume

CONTE

Le méchant sorcier Gary Bettman avait jeté un sort à la pauvre Blanche-Québec. La route vers la Ligue nationale de hockey semblait lui être interdite à jamais, encombrée de larmes et de mauvais souvenirs.

Recueillie par les sept Labeaume, Blanche-Québec recommence à rêver qu'un prince charmant la ramène dans les grandes ligues. Les siècles s'écoulent tout doucement, égayés par le comportement erratique et les sautes d'humeur des Labeaume. En attendant la venue improbable d'un prince charmant, la toute jeune Blanche-Québec s'amuse ferme en fêtant avec eux son 400e anniversaire.

Mais voilà qu'au moment où Blanche-Québec ne l'attendait plus, le prince charmant PKP apparaît au détour d'une clairière! Tout bien considéré, le Prince n'est pas exactement l'être pur et chaste dont Blanche-Québec rêvait. Il a le cœur aussi sec que le désert de Gobi et tout le romantisme d'un tiroir-caisse. Pour affronter le sorcier Bettman, Monsieur veut d'abord qu'on lui promette la construction d'un nouveau château de 400 millions $, qui portera son nom. Ensuite, il réclame tous les droits sur la future collection de lingerie fine qu'il entend bien lancer au nom de Blanche-Québec. Le Prince exige aussi qu'on lui rembourse plusieurs dépenses, notamment l'aiguisage de son épée, l'embauche d'un bataillon de joueurs de harpe pour chanter ses exploits et les frais de dentiste des 375 mercenaires qui l'accompagnent fidèlement.

Blanche-Québec hésite un peu, mais les sept Labeaume s'impatientent. Ils commencent à trouver que l'histoire a assez duré et que Blanche-Québec doit sortir de son « indolence »...

À suivre...

PAS DE MONTAGNE,
PAS D'OLYMPIQUES...
IL FAUDRAIT QU'ELLE SOIT HAUTE DE MÊME !

Roméo Labeaume & Juliette Olympique

CONTE

ui, c'est Roméo Labeaume. Un peu rugueux, mais prêt à tout. Parvenu au sommet de sa gloire, il rêve de grandeur.

Elle, c'est Juliette Olympique. Avide de sensations fortes et de comptes en banque anonymes en Suisse.

Roméo Labeaume est pressé. Il planifie le mariage pour 2022. Mais Madame trouve que leurs rendez-vous manquent singulièrement de Wow! et de Youpelaye-digidou-youpelay ! «Tu manques de relief», ne cesse-t-elle de répéter au pauvre Roméo.

Roméo Labeaume veut faire boire un philtre d'amour à sa Juliette. Mais catastrophe ! C'est son grand-oncle Marcel Obtus qui boit la potion par mégarde. Le grand-oncle se met aussitôt à dérailler, au point d'annoncer à tout le monde que c'est lui qui va se marier. Au même moment, le grand frère de Québec et le cousin d'Ottawa réalisent avec horreur que Roméo entend leur refiler la facture du mariage. Le sacripant veut aussi profiter de l'occasion pour leur faire payer le nouveau mobilier du salon et quelques ajouts à sa collection de pouliches qui sentent la framboise.

À défaut d'un mariage, Roméo Labeaume semble se diriger vers une chicane de famille carabinée. «Pourquoi en faire une montagne ?» gémit l'amoureux éconduit.

À suivre...

J'AI TOUJOURS RESPECTÉ LES GENS QUI PENSENT COMME MOI !!!

DEUXIÈME ACTE

L'AMOUR AU TEMPS DU COLÉRIQUE

SYNDIQUÉ-CROSSEUR-DE-SYSTÈME,
PERMANENT-INCOMPÉTENT,
CYBER-FLÂNEUR-DÉGUEULASSE !!!

Petit catalogue des produits fétiches d'un maire

N'écoutant que son courage, *le Petit Labeaume illustré* a mis la main sur le catalogue de produits fétiches du maire de Québec. Une fenêtre entrouverte sur les coulisses du vrai pouvoir...

Produit-vedette no 1 : Le bouc émissaire

Besoin de dénicher rapidement un coupable ? Une tête de Turc ? Besoin de blâmer quelqu'un pour vos malheurs, dans un monde où l'on jurerait que ce n'est jamais la faute de qui que ce soit ?

Du calme. Nos boucs émissaires sont là pour vous. Discrets, polyvalents, capables d'encaisser sans mot dire les pires insultes, nos coupables en or constituent un outil essentiel pour sortir de l'eau chaude.

Vous avez sans doute remarqué qu'en matière de bouc émissaire, Régis Labeaume a un petit faible pour le fonctionnaire. Au fil des mois, il a utilisé avec un certain succès nos modèles de fonctionnaire « syndiqué-crosseur-de-système », « permanent-incompétent », et « cyber-flâneur-dégueulasse ». Notons que l'efficacité de ces boucs émissaires apparaît particulièrement élevée à Québec, ville étatique par excellence, où la chasse au fonctionnaire est permise douze mois par année.

Malgré tout, n'importe qui vous dira que la qualité des boucs émissaires n'est plus ce qu'elle était. Moins durables, les boucs émissaires d'aujourd'hui s'usent vite. Il faut en changer régulièrement.

ÊTES-VOUS SÛRS DE VOULOIR PLUS DE TRANSPARENCE ?

De plus en plus, lorsqu'il cherche un coupable, M. Labeaume se tourne donc vers le journaliste, qui offre des possibilités très variées. De mémoire, citons le «journaliste qui manque de rigueur», le «journaliste qui cherche du spectacle», de même qu'un modèle de luxe, beaucoup plus rare, le «journaliste colonisé».

Cette semaine, surveillez nos spéciaux sur les boucs émissaires : achetez le fonctionnaire trop bavard et obtenez en prime une cargaison de députés fédéraux conservateurs de la région de Québec, invisibles, interchangeables et biodégradables.

Réservez tôt, car tous nos produits ne sont pas garantis en cas d'élections précipitées...

Produit-vedette no 2 : Les lunettes roses

Qui a dit que l'électeur devait tout voir ? Tout savoir ? La transparence, c'était très utile pour le cinéaste Alfred Hitchcock, lorsqu'il filmait à travers un rideau de douche, pour son film Psychose.

Mais en politique, c'est autre chose. Rien ne vaut une bonne paire de lunettes roses.

Grâce à ces lunettes ultra-performantes, les électeurs verront l'actualité d'un regard nouveau. Munies de lentilles déformantes, elles parviennent à grossir démesurément des faits sans importance, tout en rapetissant les événements majeurs.

Pour un prix modique, vous pouvez aussi fixer à la monture un petit dispositif révolutionnaire. Celui-ci interdira les regards en arrière, en plus d'empêcher toute vision d'ensemble.

Ébahi par les lunettes roses de Régis Labeaume, l'électeur ne trouve pas suspect d'accorder un contrat sans appel d'offres à Clotaire Rapaille, pour « rajeunir » l'image de la ville. Il ne voit rien d'anormal à ce que le maire abandonne brusquement l'organisation du Forum des cultures, après avoir présenté l'événement comme un *must*, les olympiques de la culture. Il ne sourcille pas non plus lorsque lorsque la Ville assume tous les risques de la construction d'un nouvel amphithéâtre.

Consultez nos spécialistes pour savoir comment combiner vos lunettes roses avec d'autres produits-vedettes comme la poudre aux yeux ou l'écran de fumée.

Produit-vedette no 3 : La porte de sortie

Ne le dites pas trop fort. Par définition, l'électeur est ingrat, exigeant et cruel.

Alors pourquoi se laisser étouffer par les scrupules? Pourquoi se laisser cuisiner comme une vulgaire pièce de viande sur le grill? Qu'on se le dise, pour se tirer d'une situation embarrassante, rien ne vaut une porte de sortie bien placée.

Le modèle le plus courant est de format réduit, lorsqu'il s'agit seulement d'esquiver une question gênante ou de faire oublier une déclaration malheureuse. Combien de fois Régis Labeaume s'est-il extirpé d'un faux-pas en brandissant notre porte de sortie : « Moi, je dis ce que je pense ». Sans oublier l'incontournable « Je n'ai pas la langue de bois ». À venir aussi, une porte de sortie fabriquée sur mesure pour le maire de Québec : « Voudriez-vous que je devienne aussi plate que le maire de Montréal, Gérald Tremblay ? »

Qu'avez-vous à perdre, après tout ?

Si les choses tournent vraiment mal, il reste encore la porte de sortie définitive. L'arme ultime, en quelque sorte. Offerte en deux modèles indémodables.

Il est vrai que la porte de sortie, « J'avais envie de relever de nouveaux défis », ne suffit plus toujours. On conseille désormais de la combiner avec la classique : « J'avais besoin de consacrer plus de temps à ma famille ».

Note : Pour en savoir plus, consultez Ignazio Silone, *L'école des dictateurs* (traduction de l'italien), Paris, Éditions Gallimard, 1981, 303 pages.

ET EN PLUS, ILS ME VERSENT 300,000 $!!!
HAHiHiHiHi...
HAHAHAHA HA HA
ARRÊTE CLOTAIRE, J'VAIS PISSER DANS MES CULOTTES !!!
HA HA

Journal imaginaire de Clotaire Rapaille

New York, le mercredi 11 novembre 2009

Trois cent mille dollars.

C'est ce que vient de m'offrir le maire de Québec, Régis Labeaume, pour rajeunir l'image de sa « Vieille Capitale ». Une jolie somme. Mais à bien y penser, j'aurais pu demander plus. Quand je lui ai fait mon petit numéro du Français béat d'admiration devant l'Amérique, il s'est tellement gonflé d'orgueil que j'ai cru qu'il allait s'envoler par une fenêtre.

Je sais. Il y a des gens qui vont trouver bizarre de consacrer 300 000 $ pour répondre à des questions existentielles du genre : « Est-ce que la ville de Québec est un homme ou une femme ? »

Il y a aussi des enquiquineurs qui feront remarquer que je ne connais pas grand-chose au Québec. Mais l'ignorance ne m'a jamais empêché de donner mon opinion sur un sujet. Bien au contraire.

L'important, me répétait toujours un roi de France dont j'oublie le nom, « c'est de jamais jouer à saute-mouton avec une licorne. »

J'avoue que plus de trois siècles plus tard, je me demande encore ce qu'il voulait dire au juste...

Québec, le mercredi 3 février 2010

Après une semaine passée à Québec, je peux certifier que cette ville constitue un endroit étrange.

Partout, je rencontre des gens qui veulent tellement me faire confiance que cela fait peur. Même les journalistes se bousculent pour participer à mes séances pseudo-pop-psychanalytiques ! Je n'en reviens pas !

C'est pas ici qu'un vieux ronchon comme Karl Kraus aurait pu dire : « La psychanalyse est cette maladie mentale qui se prend pour sa propre thérapie ».

Braves Québécois. J'ai failli leur demander d'imiter le grognement du goret qui se roule dans le lait chaud. Juste pour voir jusqu'où j'aurais pu les conduire...

Bon prince, comme toujours, je me suis contenté de les traiter de sado-masochistes. Ça les a fait réagir, mais je suis sûr qu'ils ont aimé cela, au fond. Pffff. Il n'y a qu'à voir le genre de députés qu'ils élisent, dans leur belle région de Québec, pour comprendre à quel point ils adorent se faire du mal.

Si Freud avait été Québécois... il ne se serait pas intéressé à l'Inconscient. À l'inconscience, peut-être ?

Paris, le lundi 29 mars 2010

C'est la catastrophe ! Je n'arrive toujours pas à croire que mon ami le maire Labeaume ait pu me virer pour quelques imprécisions sur mes livres et sur mes études. Dites-moi que je rêve ? Monsieur pense peut-être que le marketing et la publicité, c'est l'art de dire la vérité ? Attendez. Laissez-moi deviner. Il croit peut-être tout ce que racontent les publicités de pizzas ou de voitures ?

Si cela peut calmer tout le monde, je vais faire une confidence. Approchez-vous, je ne la répéterai pas. Plus près. Encore plus. Voilà. Vous êtes prêts?

En juillet 1608, je n'étais pas avec mon pote Samuel de Champlain, pour la fondation de la ville de Québec.

À l'époque, si vous voulez tout savoir, j'étais retenu en Europe pour négocier les droits de Galilée sur une nouvelle invention. Une affaire compliquée, je ne vous dis pas.

Bon. Vous êtes contents ? Est-ce qu'on peut tourner la page, maintenant ?

Miami, le 29 mars 2011

Un an déjà que j'ai été bouté dehors de Québec. Comme le temps passe vite.

Quand j'y repense, c'est vrai que j'étais allé un peu fort avec mes prétendus souvenirs de chansons de Félix Leclerc, en pleine guerre mondiale. Pourquoi pas des souvenirs de Michael Schumacher remportant une épreuve de Formule Un au temps des pharaons, tant qu'à y être ?

Ça ne fait rien. Un jour, les Québécois oublieront tout cela. Un jour, je reviendrai leur poser des questions existentielles. Du genre : « Est-ce que la ville de Québec se caractérise par un climat polaire ou bipolaire ? »

Tous les peuples du monde savent que lorsqu'on déboulonne un monument comme moi, il vaut mieux conserver le piédestal. Ça peut toujours resservir...

L'Histoire joue en ma faveur. Quand le Québécois a besoin de vacances, il prend la route de Miami. Quand il a besoin d'argent, il va pleurnicher à Ottawa. Et quand il a besoin de se faire dire qu'il existe, il se tourne vers la France.

REFAIRE L'IMAGE DE QUÉBEC...
PAS MAL !

250,000 $ pour Rapaille...

OUI MAIS, MONSIEUR LABEAUME, LES CRITIQUES, ÇA FAIT PARTIE DE LA DÉMOCRATIE !?!
CONGÉDIEZ LA DÉMOCRATIE !!!
VILLE DE MOI

Les Labeaumeries II

LES GRANDES CITATIONS DU MAIRE LABEAUME

« Je pourrais poser n'importe quelle question stupide. Les gens disent que c'est juste une question, mais elle est stupide ta question. C'est-tu possible qu'elle soit moins stupide ? »

– En réponse à la conseillère indépendante Anne Guérette, à l'hôtel de ville de Québec, 1er novembre 2010.

« Pis j'ai le goût de faire affaire avec les meilleurs. Je ne dis pas que Cossette n'est pas bon, mais là, on a affaire à un *king* qui parle français. »

– Interrogé sur le secret qui entourait la rémunération de Clotaire Rapaille. *Le Soleil*, 12 novembre 2009.

« Mon ostie, m'a t'en câlisser une dans l'front. »

– À l'hôtel de ville, en direction d'un conseiller municipal, Michel Fecteau. *Le Soleil*, 1er décembre 2008.

« Je vais aller la pelleter ».

– À propos de la réticence de la Commission des champs de bataille nationaux à déneiger la côte Gilmour. *Le Soleil*, 9 décembre 2010.

« Vous savez, je n'ai plus grand espoir sur la nature humaine. Je suis assez égal comme caractère. »

– *Le Soleil*, 30 mars 2010.

« Il a l'air d'un colonel de milice privée qui tente de déstabiliser un régime démocratiquement élu. »

– Commentaire sur le président de la Fraternité des policiers et policières de la Ville de Québec, Jean Beaudoin. *Le Journal de Québec*, 18 août 2008.

« J'ai promis l'amphithéâtre avec 80 % d'appuis. Êtes-vous en train de dire que les gens qui m'ont élu n'ont pas d'éthique ? »

– À un journaliste qui lui demandait si cela posait un problème éthique de construire un amphithéâtre avec des fonds publics, en période de restrictions budgétaires, *Le Journal de Québec*, 11 février 2011.

« Les incompétents nous ont fait voter ça et j'étais convaincu qu'il y avait une stratégie de communication. Mais il n'y en avait pas et ces incompétents se cachent depuis deux jours. »

– Entrevue accordé au journal *Le Soleil*, 4 novembre 2010.

HÉ LE GROS QUI LIT LE JOURNAL EN BUVANT UN CAFÉ, JE T'AI VU RIRE DE MOI !
PIS TOI AUSSI LA PETITE BRUNE QUI SE CACHE DERRIÈRE SES MOTS CROÎSÉS !

« Ça part d'une saine crainte dans toute l'organisation. Il faut que les gens craignent le maire. Ensuite, ça percole. »

– Sur les moyens à prendre pour éviter la corruption. Entrevue au *Journal de Québec*, 2 octobre 2009.

« Je pense que le député doit m'appeler pour m'expliquer un certain nombre de choses parce que ça ne peut pas fonctionner comme ça. »

– À propos des insultes publiées sur Facebook par l'attaché politique de Patrick Huot, le député libéral de Vanier. TVA Nouvelles, 11 février 2011.

« C'est tellement intelligent. (...) Moi je commence à penser qu'on va faire ça avec toutes les compagnies qui s'impliquent à Québec. »

– En réaction à une campagne menée par l'animateur de radio Sylvain Bouchard du FM-93 pour inciter les auditeurs à acheter tous les produits Red Bull dans les épiceries. *Le Journal de Québec*, 26 février 2009.

« Que les détracteurs se le tiennent pour dit. [En matière d'insultes], je me répète, j'entends préconiser la tolérance zéro. »

– Menaçant de poursuivre ses détracteurs trop virulents. *Le Soleil*, 21 février 2011.

TOUT VA MAL
À MONTRÉAL !
FAITES-MOI
CONFIANCE,
ON VA LES
RATTRAPER !

Jouons un peu

QUESTIONNAIRE

Le Petit Labeaume illustré vous propose de tester vos connaissances. Ceux qui n'obtiennent pas la note de passage doivent subir la prochaine colère de Monsieur le maire !

1) DE LA FUITE DANS LES IDÉES. En 2009, Régis Labeaume a fait de la construction d'un nouvel amphitéâtre « multifonctionnel » l'enjeu central des élections à la mairie. Il a déjà annoncé que les élections de 2013 permettraient à la population de se prononcer sur un autre projet. Lequel ?

a) La construction des éco-quartiers de la Cité verte, de Pointe-au-lièvre et D'Estimauville.

b) Un train à haute vitesse entre Québec et Windsor.

c) La construction de deux lignes de tramway de 1,5 milliard $.

d) La tenue du Forum universel des cultures en 2016, avec un budget de 100 millions $, et des travaux d'infrastructures de 2,6 milliards.

e) La reconstruction du Manège militaire à l'identique, au coût de 250 millions $.

f) La construction de tours en hauteur «artistiques» dans le centre de Québec pour camoufler le Complexe G.

g) La candidature de Québec aux Jeux olympiques d'hiver de 2022.

h) La contruction d'un « Time Square » autour du jardin Saint-Roch.

i) Le carrousel de Monsieur Caramel.

j) Les voies réservées sur certaines autoroutes de la région.

k) La nouvelle identité de la ville, pour remplacer l'expression Vieille Capitale.

l) Le retour des Nordiques.

m) Toutes ces réponses.

2) LE COIN DU PHILOSOPHE. Parmi les citations suivantes, laquelle peut être attribuée au maire de Québec?

a) J'aime beaucoup jouer la comédie, c'est tellement plus vrai que la vie réelle.

b) Tous les «sots» sont périlleux.

c) Soyez polis avec les gens durant votre ascension, vous allez les croiser durant votre descente.

d) Je n'ai plus grand espoir sur la nature humaine.

e) Il connaît aussi bien la politique qu'un cochon peut connaître la chaîne de montage robotisée d'une usine de voitures japonaises.

3) L'ART DE SE FAIRE DES AMIS (1). Associez une personnalité avec le jugement catégorique prononcé à son égard par Régis Labeaume:

a) Guy Chevrette, ex-pdg du Conseil de l'industrie forestière du Québec.

b) Maxime Bernier, député fédéral de Beauce.

c) Francis Dupuis-Déri, universitaire et militant pacifiste.

d) Danielle Roy-Marinelli, mairesse de Lévis.

e) Nicolas Sarkozy, président français.

I. Pas fiable.

II. Minable.

III. Épars. Manque de cohérence.

IV. Grand talent.

V. Y peut-y me sacrer patience?

4) *THINK BIG*. Parmi les objectifs suivants, lequel n'a pas été fixé par le maire Labeaume pour Québec?

a) Devenir la capitale de Noël.

b) Devenir la première ville aquaresponsable [au monde].

c) Devenir la Barcelone du Nord.

d) Devenir la Genève des pauvres.

e) Devenir la vitrine nord-américaine du développement durable.

5) VRAI OU FAUX? Selon une compilation effectuée par *Le Soleil*, seulement quatre conseillers de l'Équipe Labeaume ont osé voter contre la volonté du maire, à l'hôtel de ville de Québec entre novembre 2009 et novembre 2010. En tout, huit votes sur 1200.

Votre réponse:________________

6) QUI SUIS-JE? J'ai été reçu par le premier ministre du Canada, Stephen Harper, avant le maire de Québec malgré les multiples demandes de rendez-vous de ce dernier?

a) Ultraman.

b) Youppi.

c) Bonhomme Carnaval.

d) Badaboum.

e) Souris Bouquine.

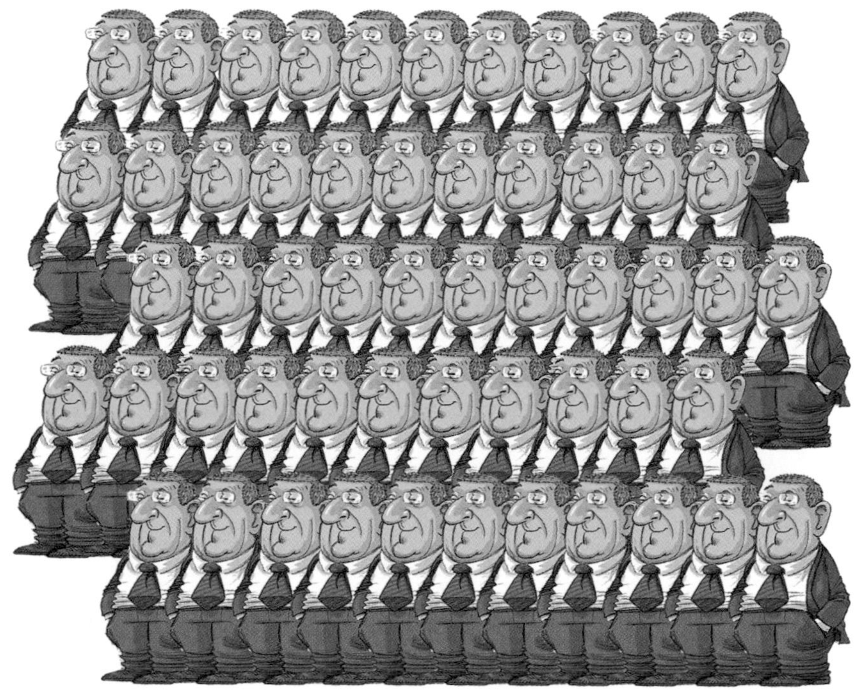

LE GROUPE CIBLE

7) UNE AFFAIRE D'ÉTIQUETTE. Comment Régis Labeaume s'est-il parfois décrit, d'un point de vue politique ?

a) Un enfant abandonné dans un magasin de bonbons.

b) Un éléphant éternuant dans un magasin de porcelaine.

c) Un social-démocrate en colère.

d) Un général qui a tendance à éparpiller ses troupes dans toutes les directions.

e) Toutes ces réponses.

8) GROUPE CIBLE. Le maire a souvent répété que toutes ses politiques visent à attirer à Québec un groupe très précis de personnes? Lequel?

a) Les gens qui ont compris que le maire et les grands projets constituaient un « package », à prendre ou à laisser.

b) Le moustachu de Brossard, qui veut payer moins de taxes et qui rêve de pouvoir enfin se déplacer rapidement en voiture, d'un bout à l'autre de sa ville.

c) Le couple de 27 à 30 ans, avec un doctorat, un diplôme de la Polytechnique de Montréal, peut-être avec un enfant. Bilingue, trilingue si possible.

d) Le couple de retraités qui se lèvent de bonne heure, qui se couchent tard et qui ne respectent pas le Guide alimentaire canadien.

e) Toutes ces réponses.

9) VRAI OU FAUX? Depuis son élection, en décembre 2007, le taux de satisfaction à l'endroit du maire Labeaume n'a jamais été inférieur à 82 %.

Votre réponse : _______________

10) L'ART DE SE FAIRE DES AMIS (2). Associez un groupe avec le jugement catégorique prononcé à son égard par Régis Labeaume :

a) Les hauts fonctionnaires municipaux.

b) Les journalistes de la télé de Radio-Canada.

c) Les citoyens du Vieux-Québec.

d) Les défenseurs du patrimoine.

e) Les partis politiques.

I. Des retraités scolarisés, des égoïstes.

II. Des incompétents.

III. Des gens qui n'ont pas « une crisse de cenne ».

IV. Rien que de la magouille.

V. Des adeptes de la télépoubelle.

QUESTION EN PRIME : LABEAUME CHEZ SMOG. Choisissez la légende qui convient le mieux avec la caricature muette.

a) « Quand j'ai commis une erreur avec Clotaire Rapaille, mon taux de satisfaction est monté à 85 %. Quand je me suis planté avec le Forum universel des cultures, il a grimpé à 92 %. À ma prochaine grosse gaffe, je franchis le cap des 100 % ! ».

b) « J'ai déjà plein d'idées pour le *Bye Bye 2011* ».

c) «Amphithéâtre, Nordiques». « Amphithéâtre, Nordiques ». « Amphithéâtre Nordiques». À Québec, si vous répétez cette prière assez longtemps, avec promesse de publier, la fée des dents Charest glisse 200 millions $ sous votre oreiller.

d) « Mon ancien psychiatre me répétait toujours : « vous êtes trop colérique ». Et quand je lui disais que j'exigeais un deuxième point de vue, il répondait : « D'accord. Vous êtes aussi mégalomane ».

e) Imaginez votre réponse :____

____

RÉPONSES

1 : g
2 : d
3 : a-V, b-IV, c-II, d-I, e-III
4 : d
5 : VRAI
6 : c
7 : c
8 : c
9 : VRAI ;
10 : a-II, b-V, c-I, d-III, e-IV
11 : La réponse est laissée à la discrétion du lecteur…

DES SONDAGES
ENCORE FAVORABLES...

Régis Labeaume et l'opposition

LE CÔTÉ OBSCUR DU MAIRE

Nous sommes en l'an 2011. Régis Labeaume règne sans partage sur la ville de Québec.

Les sondages lui prédisent un avenir radieux. Sa cote de popularité dépasse celle qu'obtiendrait Jésus-Christ dans un couvent de bonnes soeurs. Les politiciens se bousculent pour apparaître sur les mêmes tribunes que lui.

Contrairement aux maires qui l'ont précédé, M. Labeaume voyage à l'étranger sans être soupçonné de se payer du bon temps avec les fonds publics. Il peut caresser des projets ambitieux sans être accusé d'avoir des idées de grandeur. Il peut même se mettre le pied dans la bouche avec une régularité digne d'une horloge suisse, sans qu'on lui en tienne rigueur.

LABEAUME À CHICAGO
ÇA M'IMPRESSIONNE DE VOIR AUTANT DE GENS QUI NE ME CONNAISSENT PAS !
CÔTÉ

À l'hôtel de ville de Québec, le triomphe de M. Labeaume apparaît encore plus spectaculaire. Aux élections de novembre 2009, l'opposition officielle, le Renouveau municipal de Québec (RMQ), est disparue de la carte politique, en faisant moins de pshit ! qu'une pastille d'Alka Seltzer. Apparemment résigné à son sort, le parti n'avait pas osé présenter un candidat à la mairie ! Personne ne voulait aller à l'abattoir ! Il est vrai qu'en termes de dépenses électorales, Équipe Labeaume écrasait sa plus proche rivale par une marge de six contre un.(1)

Apparemment, cela ne suffit pas encore.

M. Labeaume n'est pas du genre à se contenter d'un repas gargantuesque. Il exige aussi qu'on lui serve les miettes qui sont tombées sous la table.

Lors des séances du Conseil municipal, Régis Labeaume traite les trois conseillers indépendants avec tout le mépris qu'une diva réserverait à une chorale de cowboys amateurs décimée par une épidémie de laryngite aiguë. Pendant des mois, un conseiller avait hérité d'un sobriquet qui le faisait passer pour une grenouille de sacristie. En pleine séance du Conseil, une autre se fera rappeler à quel point ses questions sont « stupides ». Remarquez, on pourra dire que le maire s'améliore. Difficile de faire pire qu'en ce jour de décembre 2008 où il avait apostrophé un conseiller d'un retentissant : « Mon ostie, m'a t'en câlisser une dans le front ».

Même à l'intérieur de l'équipe Labeaume, la main de fer de Monsieur le maire prévient le moindre faux-pas. On pense tout de suite à la remarque que réservait Charles de Gaulle à ses ministres. « J'ai entendu vos points de vue. Ils ne rencontrent pas les miens. La décision est prise à l'unanimité. »

(1) Pierre-André Normandin, « Dépenses électorales d'équipe Labeaume : six fois plus élevées que celles du RMQ », *Le Soleil*, 3 février 2010, p. 6.

83 % !!!
BEN COUDONC, CLOTAIRE RAPAILLE AVAIT RAISON !
le Soleil
83%
CÔTÉ 13-11-10

On sourit en se remémorant que Régis Labeaume avait promis d'encourager la dissidence, de ne pas abuser de la sacro-sainte ligne de parti. Le moins que l'on puisse dire, c'est que son équipe n'en a pas abusé. De novembre 2009 à novembre 2010, seulement quatre de ses conseillers ont osé voter contre l'administration. Et ils n'en ont pas fait une habitude, rassurez-vous. Sur les 1200 votes compilés par *Le Soleil*, les braves représentants d'Équipe Labeaume ont voté huit fois contre la volonté de leur maire. (2) On a même vu un conseiller qui n'osait pas donner son numéro de téléphone cellulaire à un journaliste, de peur de provoquer la colère de Monsieur le maire.

Plus docile que cela, on te cite en exemple dans les écoles de dressage de caniches.

On dira que la démocratie, ça ne se limite pas à l'hôtel de ville. Justement, M. Labeaume possède une conception très particulière de la démocratie municipale. Il lui est même arrivé de débarquer à une consultation sur « la ville idéale », en s'exclamant : « Si vous êtes venu ici pour chialer, c'est la place » ! Même chose pour la consultation sur le nouvel amphithéâtre, qui aura lieu après que le projet ait été lancé. Quand on y pense, cela laissera peut-être aux citoyens l'insigne honneur de se prononcer sur la couleur de la moquette ? Ou sur la variété de fleurs qui garnira les plates-bandes ?

(2) Pierre-André Normandin, « Équipe Labeaume : peu de chicane dans la cabane », *Le Soleil*, 8 novembre 2010, p. 4.

À défaut d'une véritable opposition sur laquelle se défouler, voilà que le maire dirige de plus en plus souvent sa mauvaise humeur sur les médias. Il paraît qu'ils réussissent même à embrouiller les explications les plus confuses. Plus grave encore, il paraît qu'ils font passer le «spectacle» avant l'information !

Ne souriez pas. Le comble a été atteint à la mi-février, lorsque le maire a menacé de poursuivre devant la justice tous ceux qui saliraient son honneur ou sa réputation...

Le maire Labeaume, qui prône la «Tolérance zéro» en matière d'insultes? N'est-ce pas l'incendiaire qui donne des conférences aux enfants sur le danger de jouer avec les allumettes? Ou le tigre qui chante les vertus de la cuisine végétarienne à l'huile d'olive?

Essayons de résumer la situation. Le match de hockey bat son plein. Équipe Labeaume mène 182 à 0. Elle affronte une équipe Pee-Wee dont les joueurs sont manchots patinant sur la bottine, dont les bâtons ont été remplacés par des flûtes à bec. La foule acclame le Capitaine Labeaume en faisant la vague d'une manière frénétique.

Et que fait le capitaine? Il pique une crise à l'arbitre parce qu'il croit avoir aperçu une poignée de spectateurs qui ne l'applaudissent pas, tout en haut, dans les balcons...

Que pourrait vouloir de plus Monsieur le maire? Peut-être un cireur de chaussures officiel?

LA VAGUE BLEUE

TROISIÈME ACTE

UN PERSONNAGE NOUVEAU, LE POLITICIEN-VEDETTE

PERSON OF THE YEAR
TIME
PSST.. CHÉRI, RÉVEILLE-TOI !
CÔTÉ 18-12-09

Technique du coup d'éclat permanent

À Québec, Régis Labeaume incarne ce qui se rapproche le plus d'une superstar locale.

Sur la rue, les passants lui réclament des autographes. On le salue comme un vieux complice. On l'encourage bruyamment, comme si on avait affaire à un athlète en train de courir un marathon. Même les enfants acclament le maire avec une ferveur qui doit rendre jaloux sa Majesté le Bonhomme Carnaval lui-même !

Avant Régis Labeaume, d'autres politiciens ont suscité l'enthousiasme, l'affection ou la sympathie. Mais le maire de Québec constitue un phénomène particulier. Monsieur construit son personnage au fur et à mesure. Il alimente un feuilleton dont il est à la fois le script et le héros. Régis Labeaume est devenu une machine à produire toujours plus de Régis Labeaume.

À Québec, les médias sont devenus complètement accros au *work in progress* du maire. On le suit pas à pas. On le pourchasse même à l'étranger, pour ne pas rater le dernier épisode. Qui s'ennuie de Virginie, quand toute une ville se raconte les derniers écarts de conduite de son maire tout étoile ?

Veut-il repeindre le Château Frontenac en bleu piscine? A-t-il bu le rince-doigts lors d'un banquet ? A-t-il mordu un invité ?

Au fond, ce que raconte précisément Monsieur le maire n'a pas toujours beaucoup d'importance. Un projet en chasse un autre. Un psychodrame en cache un autre. Forum universel des cultures. Candidature olympique. Amphithéâtre. Deux cents millions $ par ici. Quatre-vingt-six millions $ par là. Un jour, on le voit brandir une cannette de Red Bull en pleine séance du Conseil municipal, pour appuyer une compétition sportive. Le lendemain, il fait le pitre pour Infoman, en chantant *Na Na Hey Hey Kiss Him Goodbye*, vêtu d'un t-shirt des Nordiques.

La figure souriante ou grimaçante de Régis Labeaume se retrouve partout. Journaux, magazines, télévision. Impossible d'y échapper. Au fil des ans, on l'a vu brandir une pelle, pour souligner les 400 centimètres de neige tombés sur Québec, en 2008. On l'a vu jouer de la guitare, pour une école rock. On l'a vu jouer les durs, pour la promotion d'un gala de boxe. Le maire s'est aussi baladé en pelle mécanique, en auto, en bâteau, et peut-être même en maillot, qui sait ? Difficile à dire. Avec le temps, on finit par perdre le compte.

À Québec, le maire Labeaume ne monopolise pas la vie politique. Il EST devenu la vie politique. Sa seule contrainte ? L'obligation du coup d'éclat permanent. Le devoir de ne jamais passer inaperçu.

Parfois, lorsqu'il est trop contrarié, Monsieur le maire ose le grand Jeu. Il menace de se convertir à la langue de bois, comme un politicien ordinaire. Ou pire encore, il menace de taire, pour nous donner une bonne leçon. «Vous n'êtes pas habitué à ma discrétion, hein ?» a-t-il récemment demandé aux journalistes, après un silence inhabituel de quelques jours. On aurait dit une vedette qui voulait se faire supplier de donner un rappel...

L'an dernier, M. Labeaume a appris que l'équipe de l'émission Et Dieu créa Laflaque allait créer une marionnette à son image. Et comment croyez-vous qu'il a réagi ? A-t-il tenté de dissuader les concepteurs de l'émission ? A-t-il proféré des menaces ? Non, bien au contraire ! Il s'est précipité pour participer à la confection de sa propre marionnette ! Serge Chapleau et son équipe n'avaient jamais vu cela !

Gardez-vous pourtant de croire que Monsieur le maire veut faire le zouave, à n'importe quelle conditions. L'an dernier, durant la campagne électorale, un incident est venu rappeler à quel point il est sensible à son image.

Difficile à croire, mais ses sbires ont tenté de neutraliser un petit site Internet qui parodiait son équipe, rebaptisée pour l'occasion l'Équipe Embeaume. Pour justifier cette tentative de censure, ils ont suggéré que le site violait des droits de « propriété intellectuelle » !

Ils n'ont pas accusé les farceurs de plagiat, mais presque !

Il serait dommage de conclure ce chapitre sans rappeler une blague qui circulait à la même époque, à propos du maire de Québec.

Un restaurateur vend des hot-dogs aux passants, devant l'hôtel de ville de Québec. Soudain, le vent se lève, et toutes ses assiettes en carton s'envolent. Le hasard veut qu'elles passent par la fenêtre du bureau de l'infatigable maire Régis Labeaume. Le restaurateur va voir le portier et lui demande s'il peut faire quelque chose. Après un petit moment, le portier revient en lui disant qu'il ne pourra pas récupérer ses assiettes.

« Pourquoi ? » demande le restaurateur. Et l'autre répond : « Parce que le maire Labeaume les a déjà toutes signées. »

DANS CES NOUVEAUX PLANS, IL Y A UN LAC ARTIFICIEL AU MILIEU DE L'AMPHITHÉÂTRE AVEC PLEIN DE TICANARDS !

Journal imaginaire de Gary Bettman

COMMISSAIRE DE LA LIGUE NATIONALE DE HOCKEY

New York, le samedi 10 octobre 2009

Ce midi, alors que je rangeais ma collection de poupées GI Joe, le maire de Québec s'est présenté à mon bureau. Encore un autre qui rêve de la Ligue nationale ! Un certain monsieur, attendez, un monsieur Ladaboom. Non, Labeaume! Oui c'est ça! Labeaume! Et dire que mon adjointe m'avait fait répéter son nom quatre ou cinq fois, juste avant la rencontre, pour que j'impressionne le Monsieur.

C'est un truc que m'avait refilé Bill Clinton, lors d'un dîner-bénéfice en l'honneur des enfants pauvres d'un pays lointain dont je n'ai plus jamais entendu parler. Les maires des petites villes sont tous les mêmes. Vous faites semblant de connaître leur nom et ils se mettent à roucouler comme des pigeons enfermés gratis dans un silo rempli de grains.

Chaque fois, pour meubler la conversation, j'essaie de me souvenir d'une particularité locale. Ça fait des choses à dire...

Votre ville, n'est-ce pas celle qui possède une réplique grandeur nature d'un Canadian Tire construite avec des cure-dents ? Chez vous, si ma mémoire est bonne, de joyeux lurons jouent au curling en remplaçant les pierres par des poulets congelés ? C'est ça ?

Le truc, c'est de flatter leur orgueil. D'entretenir l'espoir, mais sans rien promettre. Ni pour, ni contre, bien au contraire. Apparemment, ça a fonctionné avec ce M. Ladaboom. Après notre rencontre, mon adjointe, qui baragouine le français, a entendu le maire dire à la télévision canadienne... « Bettman savait que j'existais, il me suivait. »

Glendale (Arizona), le mercredi, 15 décembre 2010

Je reviens d'une séance du Conseil municipal de Glendale, l'ennuyeuse banlieue de Phoenix où l'équipe des Coyotes tente de s'incruster. Tout ça même si la populace locale s'intéresse autant au hockey qu'aux méthodes contraceptives chez les fourmis rouges du Grand Canyon...

Mon seul regret, c'est de ne pas avoir pu contempler ma propre performance d'acteur. Un vrai triomphe.

Tout au long de la séance du Conseil, il me fallait cacher mes émotions. Surtout, ne pas montrer ma joie. Ne rien laisser paraître. En résumé, la Ville de Glendale va donner 197 millions $ à l'homme d'affaires Matthew Hulsizer, pour lui permettre d'acheter l'équipe ! 197 millions $ pour garder les Coyotes dans la grande région de Phoenix jusqu'en 2033 ! Même dans mes rêves les plus fous, je n'en espérais pas tant.

Le poisson a vraiment mordu à l'hameçon. Et moi, emporté par l'émotion, ça m'a fait penser au proverbe : « Donne un poisson à un homme, et il sera content. Apprends-lui à pêcher, et il sera heureux pour la vie. »

Bon sang ! Mais d'où me vient cet excès soudain de sensiblerie ? Faudra que j'en parle à mon thérapeute...

Raleigh (Caroline du Nord), le samedi 29 janvier 2011

C'est le week-end du Match des étoiles, et j'en ai profité pour échanger quelques bonnes blagues avec les propriétaires d'équipes. « Pourquoi est-ce qu'il n'y aurait pas de la vie sur une autre planète ? Après tout, il y en a même à Kansas City... »

Ha-ha-ha !

Blagues à part, les propriétaires sont très contents que des villes comme Québec, Winnipeg ou Kansas City fassent des efforts pour obtenir une franchise de la Ligue nationale.

Ça leur permet de faire du chantage auprès de leur ville respective. Du genre : « Si vous n'allongez pas les millions $, on déménage ! »

Bon. Il a quand même fallu que je calme le jeu, pour éviter que la machine à rumeurs ne s'emballe. « Nous n'avons aucunement l'intention de déménager une équipe, et nous ne songeons pas non plus à procéder à une expansion, » ai-je répété aux journalistes.

Donne un poisson à un homme, et il aura à manger pour la journée. Apprends-lui à pêcher, et il va s'asseoir dans un bâteau pour boire de la bière toute la journée.

C'est drôle, mais je me sens déjà beaucoup mieux.

New York, le mercredi 2 février 2010

Parfois, je m'amuse à lire les méchancetés que les intellos écrivent sur moi. On m'a même déjà comparé à un fauve en souliers vernis ! Dans un livre récent, le journaliste américian Dave Zirin me découpe en rondelles, comme on le ferait pour un vulgaire salami.

« [À son arrivée] Gary Bettman s'était vanté de n'avoir jamais mis les pieds dans un amphithéâtre de la Ligue nationale de hockey, mais de savoir comment faire « prospérer » le sport. Malheureusement, il ne connaissait strictement rien au hockey, probablement au point de penser que Guy Lafleur était le nom d'une agence d'escortes basée à Montréal. » (1)

Ha-ha-ha ! Bien envoyé. Mais qui lit ce genre de choses, je vous le demande ? Peut-être le genre de personnes qui pensent que Islanders, c'est le nom d'une marque de bâtonnets de poisson surgelés ?

(1) Dave Zirin, « Bad Sports : How owners are ruining the Games We Love », Scribner, 2010, p. 151.

New York, le samedi 12 février 2011

Les Québécois et leur maire trop bavard, ce M. Ladaboom, commencent à me taper sur les nerfs.

Je ne sais pas combien de messages ils m'ont expédiés depuis quelques jours pour signaler qu'ils vont construire un nouvel amphithéâtre multi-machin-truc à Québec.

Youhou, les Québécois ? Savez-vous depuis combien de temps Kansas City et Winnipeg se sont fait construire de nouveaux amphithéâtres, sans pour autant avoir obtenu une équipe ?

Assez, c'est assez ! Faut que je me change les idées ! Ce soir, je veux aller voir un vrai sport, avec de vrais joueurs et de vraies équipes qui jouent devant de vrais guichets fermés. Les Knicks de la NBA sont-ils en ville ?

Donne un poisson à un homme, et il aura à manger pour la journée. Apprends-lui à pêcher, et tu réussiras peut-être à t'en débarrasser pour toute la fin de semaine...

JE VOUDRAIS
RESSEMBLER À ÇA !

Le flirt avec les médias montréalais

LA SECONDE DÉCOUVERTE DE QUÉBEC

À partir de l'été 2008, les médias de Montréal sont tombés en amour avec Régis Labeaume et sa « nouvelle » ville. Pas tous, mais presque. On évoquait même à la blague la seconde découverte de Québec...

Quand on y pense, le coup de foudre était un peu prévisible. Pour mettre du piquant dans vos émissions, quoi de mieux que d'inviter le chef du plus gros village national ? Qui sait titiller un auditoire mieux que le maire Labeaume, avec son franc-parler de mononcle un peu malcommode sur les bords. Grâce à lui, la politique redevient un sport de contact. Une chose excitante, imprévisible. On jurerait que sa stratégie préférée consiste à lancer le plat de nouilles dans les airs, en espérant que quelqu'un va le rattraper à temps.

La liste des chroniqueurs et des animateurs qui ont proposé plus ou moins sérieusement d'échanger le maire de Montréal pour celui de Québec apparaît impressionnante. Même le *Bye Bye 2010* proposait un sketch intitulé « On a échangé nos maires ».

« À chaque fois [le maire Labeaume] fait des trucs et tu te dis, pourquoi l'autre (...) ne fait pas ça ? », demande Nathalie Petrowski, sur les ondes de Radio-Canada, en décembre 2009.

« Ça, c'est un maire ! Ça, c'est un gars allumé qui fait bouger sa ville ! écrit Richard Martineau dans *Le Journal de Montréal*, en décembre 2010. (...) Actuellement, au Québec, il y a des curés qui dirigent deux, trois paroisses en même temps. Monsieur Labeaume ne pourrait-il pas être maire de Québec ET de Montréal ? »

Dans *La Presse*, Patrick Lagacé raconte que la ville [de Québec] est devenue « spectaculaire », « belle », « fière », tournée « vers l'horizon ». Il trouve aussi que son maire constitue un personnage « fascinant ». « Québec a longtemps été une ville charmante, elle est maintenant devenue magnifique », résume Joseph Facal, à l'émission Bazzo.tv, à Télé-Québec, en octobre 2008.

On dit que l'amour rend aveugle, et le flirt entre les médias de Montréal et le maire Labeaume n'y fait pas exception. Les tendances autoritaires du personnage sont généralement balayées sous le tapis. Ou alors, elles sont traitées comme les petites bizarreries que l'on doit volontiers pardonner aux grands hommes. Est-ce que quelqu'un s'indignait vraiment du fait qu'Einstein ne portait pas de chaussettes?

Ceci expliquant cela, le maire de Québec est rapidement devenu un habitué des émissions de variétés, au même titre que les vedettes du cinéma ou de la chanson. On y découvre un Régis Labeaume souriant, détendu, tout miel. Presque plus vrai que le politicien. À des années-lumière du coq de village qui tempête et qui trépigne à l'hôtel de ville.

En février 2011, on a vu le maire se trémousser au son de la *Danse du smatte*, sur le plateau de l'émission En direct de l'univers. L'an dernier, on l'avait vu jouer le politicien rebelle à peu de frais à l'émission Le Verdict, avec Véronique Cloutier. « Mon conseiller aime pas ça que je vienne dans des émissions comme celle-ci, parce qu'il a peur que j'oublie que je suis maire... et que je parle trop. »

À Tout le monde en parle, Dany Turcotte, le fou du roi, lui a décerné le titre de « Napoléon de la Grande Allée ». On pouvait presque entendre le maire roucouler de plaisir.

Hélas. Vous connaissez la chanson. Les histoires d'amour finissent mal, en général. Alors peut-être que le flirt de Régis Labeaume avec les médias montréalais tournera en eau de vaisselle. Pour reprendre la boutade d'un journaliste montréalais : « On dirait que les effets du Kool-Aid que Monsieur le maire a fait boire à tous les journalistes commencent à se dissiper... »

Depuis le renvoi en catastrophe de Clotaire Rapaille, en mars 2010, il y avait du sable dans l'engrenage. Et le débat entourant la construction d'un amphithéâtre de 400 millions $, en grande partie avec des fonds publics, pourrait signifier la fin de la lune de miel.

Mais si tout se termine mal, il restera tout de même un épisode au cours duquel le maire de Québec a VRAIMENT failli intervenir dans la vie politique de Montréal.

Ça se passait quelques jours après les émeutes de Montréal-Nord, à l'été 2008. Régis Labeaume avait alors offert son aide au maire de Montréal, Gérald Tremblay, pour aller calmer les jeunes en colère. « (...) Si tu veux que je saute dans mes jeans pour qu'on aille les voir dans la rue, je vais y aller ! » aurait-il proposé. [1]

Le maire Tremblay a décliné l'offre. Mais quand on y pense, les jeunes de Montréal-Nord l'ont peut-être échappé belle. Comme on dit à Québec : « Superman, c'est pas le gars qui porte le pyjama de Régis Labeaume » ?

(1) Sara Champagne, « Régis Labeaume : fini la rivalité Montréal-Québec », *La Presse*, 15 novembre 2008.

COUDONC, QU'EST-CE QUI SE PASSE À QUÉBEC ?
ICITTE À MONTRÉAL, ON A L'AIR D'UNE GANG DE CAVES !!!
CÔTÉ 18-02-09

Conclusion

QUÉBEC EN 2060

Il était une fois un mirage. Non, attendez, ce n'est pas ça du tout. Il y a une faute de frappe. Allez, on recommence.

Il était une fois un virage. Il y a 53 ans, en 2007, Régis Labeaume avait été élu triomphalement à la mairie de Québec. Le maire Labeaume était pour la candidature de Québec aux Jeux olympiques d'hiver, pour la construction d'un nouvel amphithéâtre, pour le retour éventuel des Nordiques, pour le tramway, pour la construction d'un anneau de glace intérieur, pour les voyages à l'étranger, pour l'aménagement des berges du fleuve, pour un TGV et pour le développement d'éco-quartiers.

Jusqu'à son récent départ à la retraite, à l'âge vénérable de 99 ans, le maire Labeaume continuait à bénéficer d'un taux d'approbation fort respectable de 65 %. À peine moins que ce qu'il récoltait au faîte de sa gloire, au moment de l'annonce de la construction de l'amphitéâtre actuel. Comme il le répétait en substance : « J'aime mon public et mon public m'aime ».

Mais tout cela appartient à un passé révolu, pour ne pas dire à l'époque pré-hystérique. Aujourd'hui, un ange est passé. En 2060, le nouveau maire est viscéralement opposé à l'idée de mettre un sou dans une candidature de Québec aux Jeux olympiques d'hiver, rebaptisés les Olympiques-assiette. Monsieur s'est prononcé contre la construction d'un nouvel amphithéâtre, contre le retour des Nordiques, contre la construction d'un tramway, contre les voyages à l'étranger, contre la construction d'un toit sur l'anneau de glace, contre l'aménagement trop élaboré des berges du fleuve, contre un TGV et contre les éco-quartiers derrière lesquels il voit une conspiration écolo-bolchévique. Pour le maire, il est hors de question que la Ville de Québec assume toute seule le retour d'un jardin zoologique ou même de la tenue d'un championnat mondial de hockey.

Les derniers sondages le créditent d'un taux d'approbation de plus de 80 %.

À quel moment s'est produit le déclic, la métamorphose, le virage à 180 degrés ? À quel moment l'opinion publique de Québec s'est-elle retournée comme un gant?

Suggérons une date, qui en vaut bien une autre.

Le 1er avril 2060, le jour du Poisson d'avril, le nouveau maire avait une grande nouvelle à annoncer, sur les ondes de Radio-Canada. Le projet de complexe théâtral si cher à Robert Lepage, dans une immense cavité située sous la falaise, en plein centre-ville, était relancé. Le complexe prendrait la place de l'actuelle fondeuse à neige géante, qui générait une chute d'eau tiède, le long de la falaise. Pour calmer les opposants, Monsieur le maire affirmait que la fluoration de l'eau de la chute était devenue hors de prix !

Il s'agissait bien sûr d'un poisson d'avril, auquel le maire avait accepté de participer. Mais plusieurs auditeurs ont mordu à l'hameçon. Au point d'expédier des courriels rageurs pour dénoncer le projet.

Difficile à croire, mais un petit nombre de gens ont aussi tenu à signaler à Radio-Canada qu'ils appuyaient le projet du maire. À croire que ce dernier pouvait désormais leur faire avaler n'importe quoi.

Une nouvelle ère commençait...

LE NOUVEAU VISAGE DE QUÉBEC

HÉATRE

LIONS UNCAGED

LIONS UNCAGED

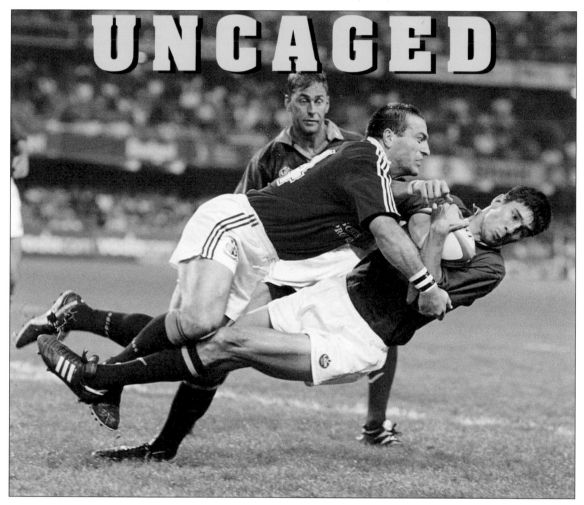

BY JOHN BENTLEY
WITH PHIL MCNEILL

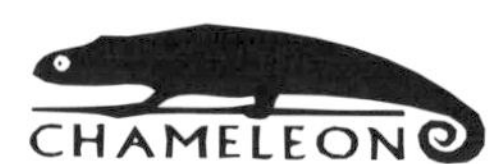

DEDICATED TO SANDY, LLOYD, MILLIE AND FAYE
BECAUSE WITHOUT THEIR LOVE AND SUPPORT
I WOULD NOT HAVE BEEN ABLE TO COMPLETE THE TOUR
– JOHN BENTLEY

Edited by Phil McNeill
Designed by Paul Sudbury and Phil McNeill
for DC Publications

With thanks to:
Catherine McNeill for interview transcriptions,
The Express Sport for use of its cuttings,
Justin Davies at Allsport for picture research,
Ken Vaughan and Graham Brown for bringing back goodies,
Joe Crowe and Natalie Froud for their assistance,
David George Crowe and Mark Peacock for the original idea,
and Tim Forrester for making it happen.

First published in Great Britain in 1997 by Chameleon Books
106 Great Russell Street, London WC1B 3LJ

André Deutsch Ltd is a subsidiary of VCI plc.

CIP data for this title is available from the British Library
ISBN 0233 99 3444

Printed by Jarrold Book Printing.

SPECIAL THANKS AND A LARGE DRAM
TO ALAN TAIT AND DODDIE WEIR
FOR LENDING US THEIR PHOTOGRAPHS

CONTENTS

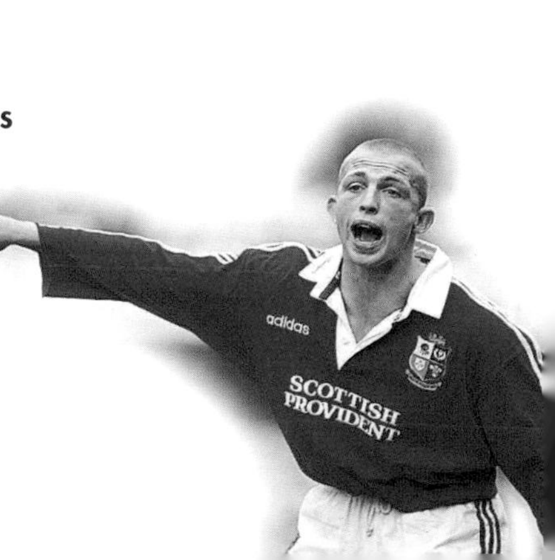

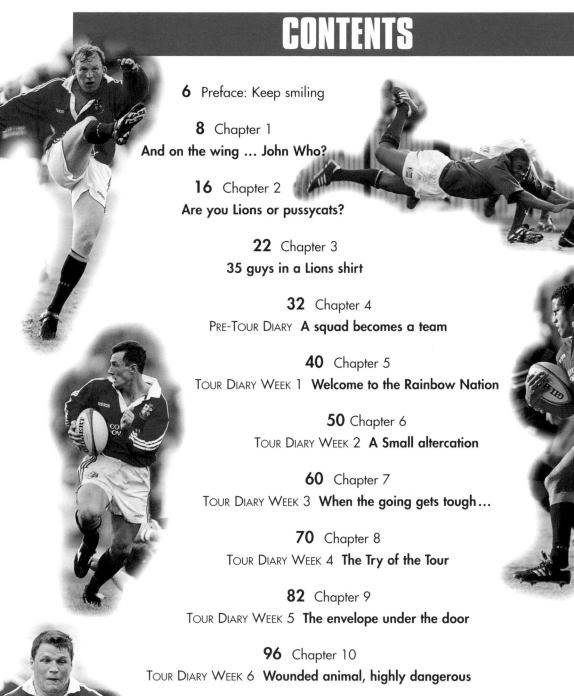

Bentley drives fans wild

Winger's brilliant run spurs on Lions

RUGBY UNION

Bentos beefs up his cult status

NICK BEAL may have grabbed the plaudits for his second-half hat-trick of tries against the Emerging Springboks but he was more than happy to share the credit with the Lions' emerging cult hero,

agreed, pointing in particular to Newcastle wing Bentley's 60-yard run which presented Beal with his first try.

Beal added: "It was another great run

we were only 16-15 ahead. But we worked hard and waited for the gaps to appear."

Fans who have arrived in South Africa for Saturday's First Test in Cape Town

HELL BENT

Bentley turbo charge

Cotton cheered by try of tour

from broken-field play and my

Bentley set to give Lions added bite

Hero Bentley rolls in to lift England

RUGBY UNION

Lions. Bentley, the 15 stone father of three, looks certain to claim a

INE UP

Bentley takes left turn to put brakes on Small

RUGBY UNION

doubt from the players' minds that this was in some way a Test team," said Fran Cotton, the

Mr Bentley's Diary

An Every Day Story of Rugby Folk

I can't remember how much it cost, but as soon as I saw it in the stationer's in Weybridge, I knew it was what I was looking for. It had to be something worthy of the job – something I could keep for a long time. A good sturdy hardback notebook with ruled pages. It was about half A4 size, with a couple of fish on the front. There was even a rubber band wrapped round it so you could keep your place. Perfect. This was going to be my Lions tour diary.

As I wrote it up every day as we travelled around South Africa, I never dreamed that I would be showing it to anyone other than my wife, Sandy, when I got home. It was just a memento. Well, not just that. It was also a way of keeping my thoughts focused – a kind of companion. *Strictly private.*

But now here it is, on the printed page, raw and unexpurgated (apart from Mr X...).

The idea of turning it into a book is to give an insight into what really goes on on tour. I made a lot of good friends, we had a lot of laughs and shared a lot of late nights, but we also worked very, very hard and we achieved what we set out to do.

I'm proud to have been a 1997 Lion and I only hope this book does justice to one of the great rugby adventures of all time.

Keep Smiling

John Bentley.

Chapter 1

And on the wing ... John Who?

NEVER HEARD of him. That must have been the reaction of most rugby union followers the day that I became a Lion. If it had been the day before, even I might have thought it was an April Fool's Day wind-up. But on April 2nd 1997 I was up long before the postman arrived, waiting anxiously for the letter that would tell me whether I was one of the 35 British and Irish Lions who would take on the world champions, South Africa.

The lead-up to that day had been dominated by the glamour boys – the will-he-won't-he-tour debate about Will Carling, which finally ended in a 'won't'; the omission of England captain Phil de Glanville, which had the Press up in arms; and speculation about who would be captain – Ieuan Evans, Rob Wainwright, Jason Leonard, Lawrence Dallaglio or possibly Martin Johnson, who most critics said had too much of a 'temperament problem' to take on such a taxing role.

Even though I was on the provisional list of 62 players which Fran Cotton, the manager, had announced in February, few rugby writers predicted I would make the final 35. Naturally, I aimed to prove them wrong. When Fran first called me, he said it was down to me whether I made the tour. I had been playing well for Newcastle – four hat-tricks in the season – and I was backing myself to be on that plane to Johannesburg.

When I opened the letter, an amazing surge of emotion shot through my body. The hairs on the back of the neck crinkled up – it was a fantastic feeling. Ever since I was a boy I had dreamed of playing for the British Lions. Now, at the age of 30, my dream was about to come true.

Yet I must confess I had mixed feelings. I had a contract to play for Halifax Blue Sox that summer in the World Club Championship and the English Super League – and I had not yet got permission from them to go on the tour. That would take some sorting out.

And, to be honest, going on the Lions trip would be a sacrifice in a couple of ways. On

Lions selection sparked a frenzy of club and country photocalls. Top: The Newcastle Lions – Alan Tait, Tim Stimpson, Doddie Weir, John Bentley, Tony Underwood. Left: The Irish Lions – Keith Wood, Eric Miller, Jeremy Davidson, Paul Wallace. Right: The Leicester Lions – Graham Rowntree, Austin Healey, Martin Johnson, Neil Back and that man Miller again

this first ever professional Lions tour, all 35 players were to be paid £10,000 each, plus a bonus of £7,500 if we won the Test series. I would have earned a lot more working for Halifax – though of course there are certain things in life that money can't provide. And secondly I would have to leave my family for eight weeks. I've got three little ones: Lloyd, who was seven on the day I left; Faye, who's five; and Millie, who was eight months old at the time. To leave them for two months would be a great commitment – and in fact that was my inspiration throughout the tour. If I was going to make that sacrifice, I was determined to play well and have a tour I could look back on with pride.

My wife Sandy said: 'You have to go', and I knew I had come too far in my long rugby career to turn the chance down now.

I REMEMBER telling my mum when I was seven years old that one day I hoped to play for England. That was when I started playing rugby union back home in Cleckheaton – a small town in the heart

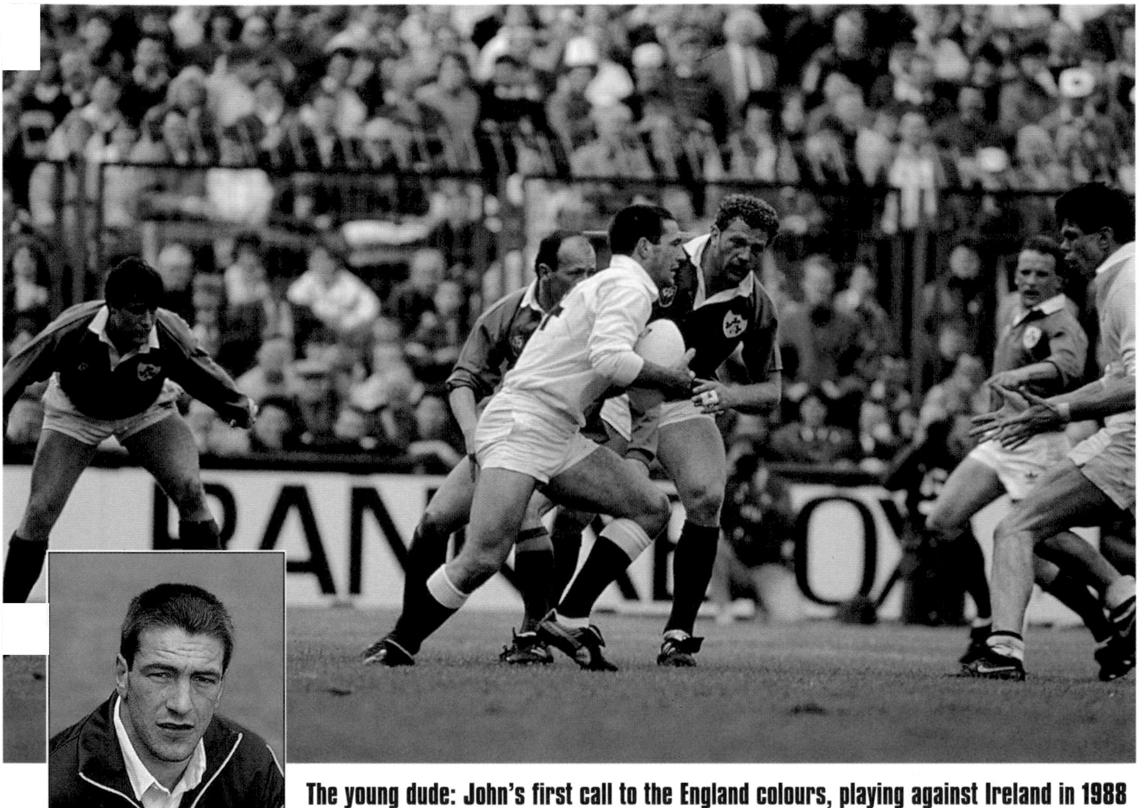

The young dude: John's first call to the England colours, playing against Ireland in 1988

of West Yorkshire, between Leeds, Bradford and Dewsbury. The great England centre Jeff Butterfield, who played 29 times for his country in the Fifties, comes from Cleck. He's a local legend, and is fondly remembered in South Africa, where he was one of the outstanding players on the Lions' tour of 1955.

Seven is very young to play rugby, but it runs in the family. I played scrum-half until I was 17. Then in a colts match Cleckheaton switched me to centre as an experiment and I took it from there.

I left Cleckheaton to play for Otley, and was picked at centre for Yorkshire. With Rory Underwood and Mike Harrison on the wings and Rob Andrew at fly-half, we won the County Championship final at Twickenham. I then signed for Sale, in the first season of the Courage Leagues.

The highlight of my early rugby union career came when I was selected for England against Ireland in April 1988. They put me on the wing, where I had never played before – but I would have played at hooker to get an England shirt on my back. I was on the right wing with Rory Underwood on the left as we won 21-10 in Dublin.

I then went on the summer tour of Australia, where I made my mark off the field ... but not on it. It was a fantastic tour for me, the only problem was the rugby didn't go too well! Later, I realised I had got my priorities wrong and I decided that if I was ever going to go on tour again, I was going to do my game justice. I'm just glad I got the chance. When *Rugby World* magazine previewed the individuals on the 1997 Lions tour, they said I 'could well emerge as the joker of the party'. Fine – but I was determined that that wasn't the only thing I would be remembered for.

In the first Test on that 1988 tour, Rory and I

PROVISIONAL LIONS SQUAD

The 62 names – 27 Englishmen, 13 Welsh, 13 Irish and nine Scots – announced by Fran Cotton on February 17 1997, who assembled in Birmingham on March 11 to be measured up for the task ahead

FULL-BACKS
Neil Jenkins (Wales)
Tim Stimpson (England)
Nick Beal (England)
Jim Staples (Ireland)
Jim Mallinder (England A)

WINGS
Adedayo Adebayo (England)
John Bentley (England)
Simon Geoghegan (Ireland)
Kenny Logan (Scotland)
Gareth Thomas (Wales)
Ieuan Evans (Wales)
Denis Hickie (Ireland)

CENTRES
Allan Bateman (Wales)
Jonathan Bell (Ireland)
Scott Gibbs (Wales)
Jeremy Guscott (England)
Alan Tait (Scotland)
Nigel Davies (Wales)
Will Greenwood (England A)

STAND-OFFS
Paul Grayson (England)
Gregor Townsend (Scotland)
Craig Chalmers (Scotland)
Mike Catt (England)
David Humphreys (Ireland)

SCRUM-HALVES
Kyran Bracken (England)
Bryan Redpath (Scotland)
Matt Dawson (England)
Austin Healey (England)
Andy Gomarsall (England)
Rob Howley (Wales)

LOOSE FORWARDS
David Corkery (Ireland)
Richard Hill (England)
Ian Smith (Scotland)
Rob Wainwright (Scotland)
Lawrence Dallaglio (England)
Martin Corry (England A)
Denis McBride (Ireland)
Eric Miller (Ireland)
Tim Rodber (England)
Scott Quinnell (Wales)
Ben Clarke (England)
Gwyn Jones (Wales)

LOCKS
Simon Shaw (England)
Martin Bayfield (England)
Garath Archer (England)
Martin Johnson (England)
Jeremy Davidson (Ireland)
Paddy Johns (Ireland)
Craig Quinnell (Wales)
George Weir (Scotland)

PROPS
John Davies (Wales)
Jason Leonard (England)
Nick Popplewell (Ireland)
David Young (Wales)
Rob Hardwick (England)
Graham Rowntree (England)
Paul Wallace (Ireland)
Tom Smith (Scotland)

HOOKERS
Mark Regan (England)
Phil Greening (England)
Keith Wood (Ireland)
Jonathan Humphreys (Wales)

both scored and we were narrowly beaten 22-16. But I was dropped for the next Test ... and didn't play for England again for nine years.

Mind you, I am still amazed that I *ever* played for England again, because by the end of 1988 I was a rugby league professional in an era when rugby union was still strictly amateur, and once you crossed that Great Divide there was no turning back. Somehow I always believed I would return to union one day, but I thought it would be for Cleckheaton on a Sunday afternoon, just to get me out of shopping with the wife.

I swapped codes because I was disillusioned with rugby union. Will Carling had been given the England captaincy and he played at centre, which was where I wanted to play – not that there appeared much chance of that, because I didn't even get selected for the North of England team. I had joined the West Yorkshire police force in June 1987, and was posted in the Headingley area of

Leeds. So when Leeds, the rugby league club I supported as a boy, came in with an offer in November '88, I took it.

People had always said I was a rugby league player in a union shirt. I played a very physical game and I adapted to league very quickly. In fact I found it far easier than when I eventually returned to union.

In my nine years in rugby league I have played for Leeds and Halifax, Great Britain and England, plus a guest season in 1994 with Balmain Tigers of Sydney. With the breakdown of the barriers between the two rugby codes, I was among the first league players to return to union. In 1996 I signed up to play union for Newcastle Falcons in the winter while still playing league for Halifax in the summer. It is a great challenge, but it means I haven't really had a break since 1993. I admit it's not the best way to carry on. The body can cope, but mentally you need time to recuperate.

Are you being served? Ieuan Evans, Lawrence Dallaglio and Scott Quinnell get measured up for their Lions blazers, shirts and tracksuits

When I first played for Newcastle I found it surprisingly difficult. To be honest, I had thought I would be a sensation, having played rugby league at such intensity, but it's a completely different game. In rugby league, when you get tackled the game stops. In rugby union, that's when the game starts! I kept making the mistake of isolating myself by going too far and losing possession. It was frustrating, and even when I joined the Lions I was still learning certain aspects of the game.

Newcastle have been fortunate to have the same owner as Newcastle United, Sir John Hall, and they've taken the professionalism of the football club into the rugby setup. Playing there certainly helped me get into the Lions because we were beating teams every week. If we had been losing I don't think I would have been considered.

When Fran first contacted me, he stressed that he ought to be looking at me playing against better opponents. No disrespect to some of the clubs in the Second Division, but they weren't giving Newcastle much opposition. In the event, Newcastle had five players in the 35-man Lions squad. The only club with more was Leicester, who had six, while Northampton also had five.

One of the other Newcastle players making the trip was my old rugby league adversary Alan Tait, who would be competing for a place in the backs with three other rugby league men – Allan Bateman, Scott Gibbs and me. The management's decision to go for so many guys with rugby league experience was no coincidence.

IT DIDN'T actually surprise me when I got the call from Fran Cotton so early in my union comeback. People raised eyebrows that I had not been considered for England yet was picked for the British Lions. But it's horses for courses. For whatever reason, the England management thought I was not ready for the 1997 Five Nations championship. Perhaps they were planning for the 1999 World Cup and thought I would be too old. Perhaps it was because I had not long returned to rugby union, and had not experienced the intensity of playing in the First Division.

But the British Lions were going on a seven-week jaunt to South Africa to do one job, and that

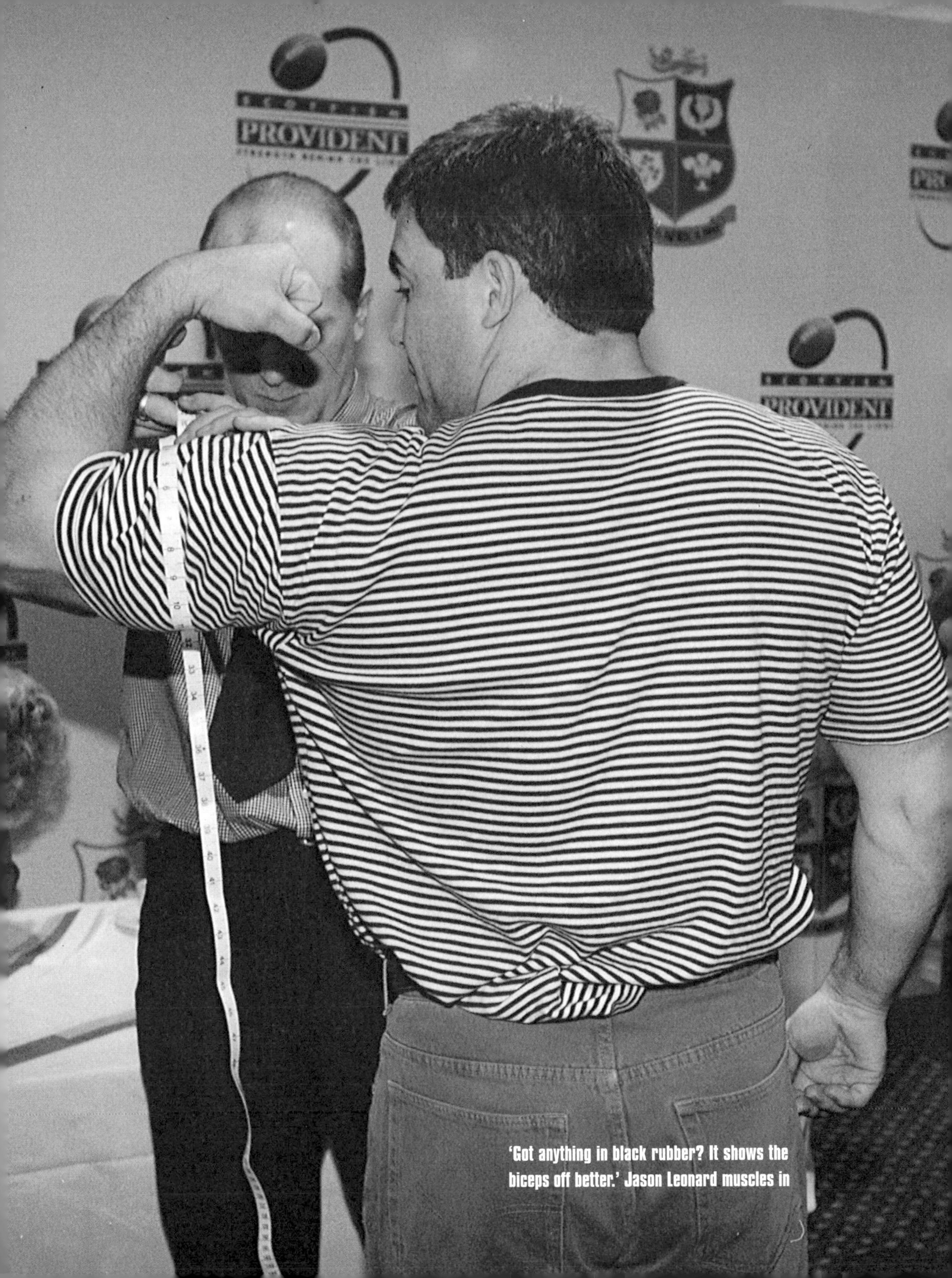

'Got anything in black rubber? It shows the biceps off better.' Jason Leonard muscles in was to win the Test series. Fran, having been down to South Africa to do a recce, and having toured there before, knew that it was one of the most intimidating places to go and play rugby. With the return of the rugby league players, he and coach Ian McGeechan felt that we would have a massive contribution to make – and they sang the same tune throughout the tour.

We had been professional for a long time. What is being professional? It doesn't just mean that you get paid for what you do. Professionalism is all about attitude and self-discipline – the way you handle yourself both on and off the field.

I had a significant input at Newcastle when I first went there and at the Lions' first training session at London Irish we trained with the intensity with which we desired to play – which was a bit of a surprise to some of the rugby union lads. I'm not saying they didn't train well, but when it's on it's on and we trained very professionally and very hard.

I can have a laugh with the best of them, but when it comes down to training you've got to concentrate and get stuck into it. That's the rugby league way. We knew this tour was going to be won or lost not just on the field of play but on the training ground, in the tactical talks at every team meeting, and even in the early hours of the morning in the hotel bar.

The rugby league connection: Scott Gibbs, Allan Bateman and Alan Tait were selected to bring a tough physical approach to the Lions' back play

Because if we were going to overcome the might of the South Africans on their own territory, we would have to have a team spirit and self-belief that were second to none.

THE RUN-UP to the start of the tour was very frustrating because there was a huge backlog in the club fixtures. Mark Evans, Saracens' director of rugby, complained: 'It is just a nonsense. By the end of the season the players are going to be out on their feet – and to think they are going to leap straight on a plane for South Africa is ludicrous.'

There were some vital matches coming up and Newcastle obviously had to get into the First Division. The Lions were due to meet up on May 12 for a week of pre-tour preparation before flying out to Johannesburg on May 17 – and as the season dragged on to the end of April, the injury list was mounting up.

Members of the Lions squad who sustained injuries in the last weeks of the season included Tony Underwood (T.U. broke his jaw playing for Newcastle), Tim Rodber, Jeremy Davidson, Keith Wood, Neil Jenkins (who broke his arm against England), Paul Grayson, Ieuan Evans and Peter Clohessy – who pulled out two days before the May 17 get-together and was replaced by his fellow Irish prop Paul Wallace.

'Any questions from the media?' 'Mr Cotton, in the run-up to the tour, will the Lions management be holding as many training sessions as press conferences?' 'Errr, no.'

The papers were full of reports about how we would be going out to South Africa completely knackered from the gruelling English season. Newcastle, for instance, finished with seven League Two fixtures in 28 days. Martin Johnson, the press pointed out, had played 44 matches without a break for England and Leicester (and he didn't have the extra burden of playing for a rugby league team on top!).

My Newcastle boss Rob Andrew told *The Express*: 'You can't have our season followed by a two-month trawl around South Africa. There will be massive burn-out of top players, because the physical nature of the sport is far greater than it has ever been.'

So there we were, the walking wounded. It seemed that no one gave us a chance. Joel Stransky, the South African fly-half who had been watching British rugby at close range with the Pilkington Cup-winners Leicester, dismissed our chances. 'I believe South Africa will win the series 3-0,' he said. 'The Lions will be fatigued and will do exceptionally well to win one Test.'

The Lions coach, Ian McGeechan, complained: 'This is my third Lions tour and it's likely to be the toughest – yet I've had the least preparation of the three.'

It probably sounds unbelievable, but the only time we all met up before the tour was when we got measured for our blazers. On March 11, all 62 of us on the provisional list travelled to Birmingham, where we met up at the Hotel Metropole at the NEC. I remember that the Newcastle lads were all late, because we got tied up in the traffic.

Still, it was a good day. We had to get fitted up for our No.1's – that's the official blue blazer, tie, shirt, trousers and shoes. On top of that we would be supplied with another pair of shoes, a pair of chinos, a casual jacket, casual tie, four shirts, a load of tracksuits, training gear, shorts ... everything you could possibly think of. We were told that, if selected, we wouldn't need to turn up with anything except underpants.

As I drove out of Cleckheaton on May 12 to go and join up with the British Lions squad, I couldn't help thinking that it was going to be quite a sight – 35 guys arriving at this smart hotel in Surrey with just their underpants on...

CHAPTER 2

Are you Lions or pussycats?

NO CHANCE, mate. That, in a nutshell, was how the world rated our prospects. And to be honest, back in April I found it hard to disagree. I remember how people used to congratulate me on being selected. They would slap me on the back, all smiles, and then say: 'Rather you than me. It's an intimidating place. You'll get your arse kicked.' If that's what my friends thought, what about the enemy?

To say the South Africans were confident is an understatement. One Cape Town newspaper carried the headline: 'THESE ARE NOT LIONS BUT PUSSYCATS'.

Joel Stransky and François Pienaar, who had been playing here with Leicester and Saracens, were writing in the South African papers saying, 'We have played among most of these players and they are nothing to fear – three-nil to the Boks.'

Stransky outlined his reasons in *The Express*. 'South Africa are extremely talented,' he said. 'They will be peaking in their fitness and playing the game at one heck of a speed against opponents who are a bit fatigued. The Lions will be doing exceptionally well to win one Test, and must expect to lose one or two provincial games as well.'

That view wasn't only held by South Africans. Many people here were saying we would lose 3-0. William Hill had South Africa as 5-1 on to win the series. Our own coach, Ian McGeechan, warned that the 13-match itinerary would be 'like playing ten Five Nations matches and three World Cup Finals'.

After all, South Africa were the world champions, playing at home on the grounds where they had won their title in front of their impassioned, rugby-mad fans. And they had only ever lost two series at home.

THE SOUTH Africans' most famous home defeat had come in 1974, at the hands of the legendary Lions team led by Willie John McBride. The Lions had come away 3-1 winners with a first team that also happened to include the Lions' current manager Fran Cotton in the front row of the scrum and coach Ian McGeechan at centre. (Not to mention JPR Williams, JJ Williams, Phil Bennett,

World champions: François Pienaar receives the cup from Nelson Mandela. Inset: André Joubert and Os du Randt

'When I saw the President walking towards me in a Springbok jersey I knew this was a victory far more important than any on the rugby pitch. When Mr Mandela chose to wear my shirt, it symbolised the coming together of a nation. The new South Africa was actually born then.'

– FRANÇOIS PIENAAR

'It hasn't been some sort of lifetime's ambition to captain the Lions. Anyone who can go abroad with the Lions and win needs to be a pretty special character, like Willie John McBride in 1974. Lack of captaincy experience does not bother me. I have four guys in the squad who have all captained their countries – Jason Leonard, Ieuan Evans, Keith Wood and Rob Wainwright – and I look forward to working with them.'

'I don't mind speaking to the Press. They ask the same questions 50 times over.'

– MARTIN JOHNSON

Fergus Slattery, Roger Uttley, Gordon Brown and Gareth Edwards...) Rightly or wrongly, they had all defied fierce anti-apartheid protests in Britain to write their names in rugby history, scoring 10 tries to South Africa's one during the series.

Since then, however, the Lions' touring record did not make happy reading:

1977 – Phil Bennett's team unexpectedly lost 3-1 in New Zealand.

1980 – Bill Beaumont's team were ambushed 3-1 by Morné du Plessis' Springboks.

1983 – Ciaran Fitzgerald led his men to a 4-0 whitewash at the hands of Andy Dalton's All Blacks.

1989 – A win at last! Finlay Calder's mob of veteran scrummagers like Paul Ackford and Mike Teague beat Nick Farr-Jones's Australia 2-1 in a series that also made Jeremy Guscott an overnight star.

1993 – Back to losing ways. Gavin Hastings' team went down 2-1 to an All Blacks side driven by the unerring kicking of Grant Fox.

Not a record to inspire confidence. On top of that, we were always being told how much better, fitter, faster, stronger, Southern Hemisphere rugby was compared to that in Britain. The very fact that Stransky and Pienaar – South Africa's World Cup-winning playmaker and captain – were here in England rather than back home playing for their country sent a shiver down the spine. As Fran Cotton said: 'Any side that can consider dropping François Pienaar must be pretty formidable.'

Judging by their recent form, South Africa had had little trouble adjusting to life without two of their biggest names. They approached the series with six straight victories including a 37-20 demolition of Wales in Cardiff orchestrated by superstar scrum-half Joost van der Westhuizen. And they would go on to give us a reminder of their power with a 74-10 thrashing of Tonga two weeks before the first Test.

It was quite a team. Their forwards have always been man mountains. Loose head prop Os du Randt – 'the Ox' – was as big as they came, and skilful with it. In

HOW THE BOOKIES SAW IT

3/1 Lions to win Test series
4/5 Lions to lose all three Tests
1/5 South Africa to win series

William Hill's odds at the start of the tour

'If the Lions are lucky they might get the last Test'

RUGBY WORLD **Rugby World magazine asked six experts to pick the winners. Their verdict was bad news for the Lions**

GARETH CHILCOTT

England & British Lions 1989

2-1 TO SOUTH AFRICA

'South Africa will edge it because with their Super 12 and Tri-Nations they're used to a high level of rugby. For the Lions to produce three huge Test performances in three weeks is asking too much. There are a lot of places up for grabs – and successful teams know their line-up from the start. They'll fall at the last hurdle.'

NAAS BOTHA

South Africa 1980-92

2-1 TO SOUTH AFRICA

'It's tough to say who will be favourites. The Lions can put 15 guys on the field who will make it tough for South Africa. But it's home advantage so maybe it's a 51-49 home series.'

ROBERT JONES

Wales & British Lions 1989, 1993

2-1 TO SOUTH AFRICA

'The Cape Town Test will be their first Test against the Lions for 17 years: it will be a big occasion for South Africa. In Wales last year they were a class above anything in the Northern Hemisphere. They have quality in depth. They're very physical – it's a good thing the Lions are taking 35 players because the intensity of the rugby will make injuries inevitable. South Africa have a lot of power and hate losing, but I think the Lions can sneak one Test.'

JOEL STRANSKY

South Africa 1993-

3-0 TO SOUTH AFRICA

'The South Africans play at a level above what the Lions are used to. Martin Johnson will win his lineout ball and the Lions have great strength at centre. The glaring weakness is at fly-half. Townsend can rip defences to bits but in a tight game he may struggle. If the Lions are lucky they might get the last Test, but South Africa will win the first two because the Lions won't have had time to adjust to that level of rugby.'

DICK BEST

Lions assistant coach 1993

2-1 TO SOUTH AFRICA

'We're at the tail end of a long, hard season. The itinerary is hard and people will be missing for the Tests because top players always get injured in South Africa. Take two or three out of the Lions' side and they've got problems.'

... And the one who got it right!

SYD MILLAR

Ireland & British Lions 1959, 1962, 1968; Lions manager 1974

2-1 TO THE LIONS

'It's all about pressure and how the players react, and Franny & Co know all about that. South Africa have a very strong defence but we can play wider. If we stretch it, the Lions can tip the balance.'

Man in the hot seat: Carel du Plessis became coach of South Africa at 36, with almost no coaching experience

the second row there was the lineout master Mark Andrews, who would probably be paired with the fearsome Kobus Wiese. Behind the marauding back row of Gary Teichmann, André Venter and Ruben Kruger there were the lightning reflexes of van der Westhuizen and the strong running of fly-half Henry Honiball. Outside them there were hard-driving centres André Snyman and World Cup star Japie Mulder. And at the back there was the 'Rolls Royce of full-backs', André Joubert.

BUT THE biggest challenge of all, as far as I was concerned, was the guy lurking out on the left wing – James Small, the bad boy of South African rugby, variously known as the Springboks' answer to David Campese or a rugby version of Paul Gascoigne. The man with the most Test caps in South African history. The man who faced up to Jonah Lomu in the World Cup Final. A man with a reputation for dirty play and more lip than Muhammad Ali. I couldn't wait to get to grips with him...

The one possible chink in the South African armour was the inexperience of their new coach, Carel du Plessis. Since Kitch Christie's team won the World Cup, the Springboks had had a bumpy ride. Christie's successor, André Markgraaff, shocked South Africa by dropping Pienaar and Stransky. He then lost a home series for only the second time in South Africa's history, against Sean Fitzpatrick's rampant All Blacks. But his team came back fighting by soundly beating France, Wales and Argentina, and were building strongly towards the Lions' visit when catastrophe struck.

At the start of 1997 Markgraaff was fired in disgrace after he was taped making racist remarks.

'I don't think the Lions will win one Test. Two defeats and a draw would be a good result for the Lions.' – *BOB DWYER, Former Australia coach*

Enter du Plessis. When he was a player, the South Africans called him the Prince of Wings. Many said he was their best winger of all time even though, due to South Africa's apartheid isolation, he played only seven internationals, and not one against the team who first inspired him ... the British Lions.

Du Plessis was 14 when he saw Willie John McBride's Lions clinch the 1974 series with a 26-9 victory in a ferocious match at Boet Erasmus stadium in Port Elizabeth. 'I thought they were an excellent, excellent team,' he said. 'To this day if you think about the '74 Lions you think about what a great team they were. The names trip off the tongue: Gerald Davies, JJ Williams, Ian McGeechan, Phil Bennett, Gareth Edwards...'

In the eyes of those who saw him, du Plessis had the skill to become a legend in his own right. But in 1989, aged only 29, after a season in which he set a Western Province try-scoring record, he retired to begin a successful career in financial services. For seven years he had almost no involvement in rugby ... until Markgraaff last year enlisted his assistance as technical adviser. When Markgraaff departed under a cloud, du Plessis found himself in the hot seat at the age of 36.

Ever the idealist, the blue-eyed Mel Gibson lookalike vowed that his team would 'develop a multi-faceted style of attacking, winning rugby in which South Africa will be innovators in the world game. I hope I can encourage the team to play with flair and a bit of risk.'

Ambitious aims for a man with almost no coaching experience who would only have one game in charge before facing the Lions. The big question was: Would Markgraaff's steam-roller respond to du Plessis' more subtle hand on the steering wheel?

It wasn't something that appeared to bother the South African public as they arrogantly wrote off our chances. But as the Lions gathered at Weybridge, there was a definite feeling that we were about to put the cat among the pigeons...

'This is probably the toughest Lions tour in history. There is a gentle three-game start, although gentle is a relative term, and then things really hot up. Every state wants a crack at the Lions. The sun, the hard grounds and the altitude all make life a different proposition to Europe.'

– FRAN COTTON, Lions tour manager

THE ITINERARY

Sat	May 24	**Eastern Province**	Port Elizabeth
Wed	May 28	**Border**	East London
Sat	May 31	**Western Province**	Cape Town
Wed	June 4	**Mpumalanga**	Witbank
Sat	June 7	**Northern Transvaal**	Pretoria
Wed	June 11	**Gauteng Lions**	Johannesburg
Sat	June 14	**Natal**	Durban
Tues	June 17	**Emerging Springboks**	Wellington
Sat	June 21	**SOUTH AFRICA**	Cape Town
Tues	June 24	**Free State**	Bloemfontein
Sat	June 28	**SOUTH AFRICA**	Durban
Tues	July 1	**Northern Free State**	Welkom
Sat	July 5	**SOUTH AFRICA**	Johannesburg

Chapter 3

35 guys in a Lions shirt

...PLUS FIVE REPLACEMENTS AND 12 MANAGEMENT. JOHN BENTLEY'S THUMBNAIL SKETCHES OF HIS FELLOW TOURISTS, WARTS, PIMPLES AND ALL

MARTIN JOHNSON
England & Leicester
Lock. Age 27 (at start of tour)
Alias: Johnno. Martin wasn't the same kind of captain as Willie John McBride, who was an inspirational character both on and off the field. He himself admits that he's pretty boring! He's not very imposing off the field. He's cautious of people and doesn't give too much away. He's very reserved and softly-spoken, but he led by example, by the way he played. He had the luxury of being surrounded by some influential players, some strong personalities who were all very constructive. The management obviously had to pick a captain for the British Lions who was certain to play in every Test – which he did, quite magnificently.

NEIL BACK
England & Leicester
Flanker. Age 28
Alias: Backy. A tremendous player who had always battled against people telling him he's too small. But the way we played the game in South Africa suited his style. A pretty smart, cool character away from the rugby field as well. A sharp dresser who likes to show his biceps off in tight-fitting T-shirts that are a couple of sizes too small for him.

ALLAN BATEMAN
Wales & Richmond
Centre. Age 32
Alias: Batman. Tremendously unlucky not to get a start in one of the Test matches. Recovered well from a hamstring injury which threatened to have him sent home. A very quietly-spoken player who would give everything for his team-mates and lived life to the full. One thing that amused me was that everybody thought he was me. I took the piss out of him because I never met anybody who thought I was Allan Bateman. He got it nearly every time we went out. Mind you, he never played it down, he let them all buy him drinks. It's just a good job he behaved himself...

NICK BEAL
England & Northampton
Wing. Age 26
Alias: Bealer. On tour he played winger, centre and full-back, which I think is his best position. He is an absolute side-splitter doing *The Life of Brian*. He knows it inside out and would recite all the parts on many occasions, usually when having had a drink.

MARTIN JOHNSON

NEIL BACK

ALLAN BATEMAN

NICK BEAL

LAWRENCE DALLAGLIO

JEREMY DAVIDSON

MATT DAWSON

IEUAN EVANS

SCOTT GIBBS

PAUL GRAYSON

WILL GREENWOOD

JEREMY GUSCOTT

LAWRENCE DALLAGLIO
England & Wasps
Flanker. Age 24
Alias: Lawrence Bowleggio, because you could drive a bus through his legs. I established a very good relationship with Lawrence. When there was an opportunity to have a drink and relax, we weren't too far apart. He had a very successful tour and gave 100 per cent. One of the unsung heroes.

JEREMY DAVIDSON
Ireland & London Irish
Lock. Age 23
Alias: Buzz Lightyear, because of his jaw. It looks like he's chewing a mouthful of marbles. He was one of the real success stories, ousting Simon Shaw for a second row place. Like all the Irish he had a good tour all round.
The Irish certainly know how to enjoy themselves and he epitomised the spirit of the touring party.

MATT DAWSON
England & Northampton
Scrum-half. Age 24
Alias: Dawse. At one point probably fourth choice for England at scrum-half and became first choice Lion. Unfortunately, not how he would have chosen but through Rob Howley being injured. He roomed with Keith Wood in the first week of the tour and Woody had some snippers, so Dawse asked for a trim. Woody promptly shaved all his hair off. Took his chances well. When Matt scored in the first Test I don't think anyone could believe it – including him.

MATT DAWSON

IEUAN EVANS
Wales & Llanelli
Wing. Age 33
Got a bit of stick for being the grandad of the party. It was a big decision for Ieuan to come on tour because his girlfriend had just had a baby. It was his third Lions tour and he had to wrestle with himself as to whether he could get suitably motivated. Some of the Welsh boys used to take the mickey out of him about his moods, because we never knew whether he had brought his Mexican happy hat with him. A great asset to the squad – it was disappointing when his tour ended with an injury.

SCOTT GIBBS
Wales & Swansea
Centre. Age 26
Alias: Snake. Played an extremely inspirational tour through his tenacious defence. Described by Jerry Guscott as the fastest prop in the game. He relishes the physical challenges. A very good guy who was on the entertainments committee with me. Blind as a bat, unbelievably. He struggles under floodlights. I had never realised that, but it's certainly something I'll remember next time I play him – the ball will be up in the sky all the time.

PAUL GRAYSON
England & Northampton
Fly-half. Age 25
Alias: Grace. He hadn't played for quite a long time before the tour and sadly he wasn't fit enough. Celebrated his 26th birthday in memorable style in Cantina Tequila in Cape Town after we had beaten Western Province. It was one of those places where the shorts are slammed down and his birthday treat was a sore head.

WILL GREENWOOD
England & Leicester
Centre. Age 24
Alias: Shaggy, because he looks like the character in *Scooby Doo*. Will suffered a bad injury against Orange Free State which cut his tour short and there were genuine fears for his life at one stage.
He was a tremendous tourist for a young uncapped player and he has a great future. He wasn't intimidated either by the people around him or by the opposition and the playing environment.

JEREMY GUSCOTT
England & Bath
Centre. Age 31
Alias: Jack, as in I'm All Right Jack. That's why he has the word JACK on his gumshield. Very straight talking, abrasive at times. But I had the utmost respect for the way he says what he thinks.
A fantastic player. He handles the press coverage very well, and the players make sure he keeps his feet on the ground – though it was hard to suppress him after he dropped that goal to win the second Test.
His wife Jayne had their third child while he was on tour; missing that must have been hard.

AUSTIN HEALEY
England & Leicester
Scrum-half. Age 23
Alias: The Gimp. For his misdemeanours on tour he was stripped to his underpants and an apple was stuck in his mouth and tied to his head with electrical tape, in a re-creation of the scene in *Pulp Fiction*. No doubt about it, he was irritating. I used to joke

AUSTIN HEALEY

RICHARD HILL

ROB HOWLEY

NEIL JENKINS

JASON LEONARD

ERIC MILLER

SCOTT QUINNELL

MARK REGAN

TIM RODBER

GRAHAM ROWNTREE

SIMON SHAW

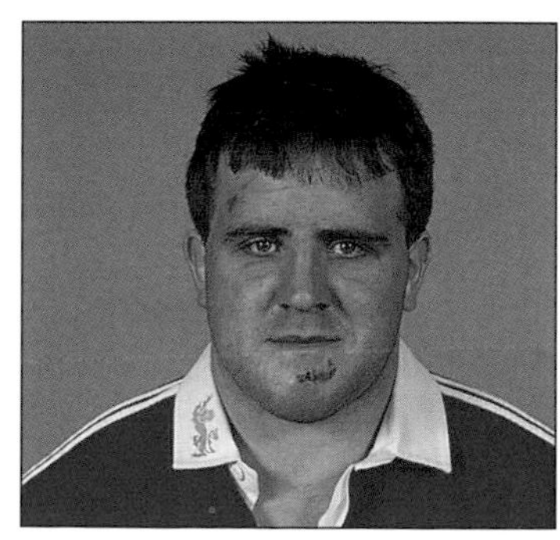
TOM SMITH

that by half past four every day I had had enough of Austin, so I wouldn't talk to him after that. He's a typical scrum-half: he likes to get under people's skin ... but he does it both on and off the field. A fantastic character and a great credit to the squad.

Richard Hill
England & Saracens
Flanker. Age 23
Alias: Hilda. Celebrated his 24th birthday on tour. He's a whinger who enjoys a good moan. Some of the more experienced players allowed him to do that so that he would feel better. He moaned about anything. If the food was too hot he moaned that it was too hot, if it was too cold he moaned that it was too cold. He just loved a moan. But he had a good tour.

Robert Howley
Wales & Cardiff
Scrum-half. Age 26
Alias: Peter Perfect. It's devastating when any player gets injured. Rob was expected to play in all the Test matches, but had to go home with a shoulder injury, which was a very emotional moment. Sadly, he wasn't really on the tour long enough to make much of an impact off the field.

Neil Jenkins
Wales & Pontypridd
Fly-half/full-back. Age 25
Alias: The Fruitbat, because of the remarkable similarity in appearance. Worth his place in any side with the way he kicks goals. A crazy guy, considering he is 25 years old and does what he does for a living. On the field he needs to be absolutely focused, yet away from the field he's crackers – very laid-back and enjoys the crack with the boys. A fantastic tourist.

Jason Leonard
England & NEC Harlequins
Prop. Age 25
Alias: Leopard. One of the seasoned campaigners, a Cockney. He has a growth in a strange place which he's pretty proud of. He calls it Scalamander and takes great pleasure in showing it! When the squad was selected he was in most people's Test sides. But he handled his disappointment very professionally and was very supportive both to the players who played in his position and to the remainder of the squad.

Eric Miller
Ireland & Leicester
No 8. Age 21
Youngest man on tour and one of the unluckiest. Would have played in one of the Tests but for the misfortune first of illness, when a virus went through the squad, then of injury. Like all the Irish lads, he had a good tour.

Scott Quinnell
Wales & Richmond
No 8. Age 24
Alias: Scotty. Comes from a great rugby-playing family. Unfortunately his tour was cut short by injury.

Mark Regan
England & Bristol
Hooker. Age 25
Alias: Ronnie. Popular for his little sayings. Instead of saying 'All right, mate', he would call people skin or babs. He comes from the West Country – 'Ooh arrr, ooh arrrr' – and obviously it was great for morale when we took the piss out of his accent.

Tim Rodber
England & Northampton & Army
No 8. Age 27
Alias: The Brigadier. Had a very good tour and played in the Tests. A mature character, he was a steadying hand through his experience both with the Army and his rugby. Was laid low early on with a virus, but he relished the style the Lions played and enjoyed playing under his club coach, and it brought the best out of his game.

Graham Rowntree
England & Leicester
Prop. Age 26
Alias: Wiggy, because of his ears. A copy of the porn mag *Club International* went round, and he was the month's sports personality, featured on Page 3 – and it made a big deal about his ears. In terms of Test selection he had a disappointing tour but remained very supportive. He nearly killed me in a go-kart accident. If it had been another winger or a centre, I would have thought it was intentional, but he was very upset about it. He was pretty impressed about being in *Club International*, but would have preferred the centrefold.

GRAHAM ROWNTREE

Simon Shaw
England & Bristol
Lock. Age 24
Alias: Shawsy. He has a more imaginative nickname but it's unprintable. Again, one who was expected to play in the Tests and didn't, but he handled that admirably. He looks intimidating, so it was very funny when he dressed up in the court session as one of the Village People.

Tim Stimpson

Alan Tait

Gregor Townsend

Tony Underwood

Rob Wainwright

Paul Wallace

Doddie Weir

Barry Williams

Keith Wood

David Young

Mike Catt

Kyran Bracken

Tom Smith
Scotland & Watsonians
Prop. Age 25
Alias: The Silent Assassin. A very, very quiet person. He played in all three Tests but I don't think I spoke three words to him all tour. He's a sleepwalker – luckily I didn't room with him!

Tim Stimpson
England & Newcastle
Full-back. Age 23
Alias: Stimmo. Suffered a very serious setback at the beginning of the tour when he had to overcome a serious pimple on his nose, which he got a lot of mick taken out of him for. Worked extremely hard on his goal-kicking. Met the best-looking girl in South Africa, but that was after he got rid of the pimple. I think she has come over to England since, so they must have had something in common.

Alan Tait
Scotland & Newcastle
Centre. Age 32
Alias: Taity. Whereas the majority of us went on tour with the aim of getting into the Test side, Taity went to South Africa with the aim of building up his biceps.
He enjoys all the posing weights and got a lot of the boys at it.
A bit of a Seventies man, he never misses the opportunity to get up and dance when any disco music comes on. Played out of position on the wing in the Tests, at my expense in the first one – bastard!

Gregor Townsend
Scotland & Northampton
Fly-half. Age 24
Alias: Toony. A quiet Scotsman who is a big book reader and enjoys organising all the little party games round the dining table – guessing games like Who's Coming To Dinner, and word games like Balderdash. I don't know what he was reading, but it certainly wasn't *Mayfair*.

GREGOR TOWNSEND

Tony Underwood
England & Newcastle
Wing. Age 28
Alias: TU. Not Underpants! Doesn't drink beer. Not a big drinker at all, but joins in on occasion, when he will have the odd blowjob – a blowjob being a short, I hasten to add. His wife was expecting their first child at home, so it was a tough tour for him emotionally, but she's doing well and he finished off a good tour playing in the final Test.

Robert Wainwright
Scotland & Watsonians
No 8/Flanker. Age 32
Didn't have a nickname, he was just a boring sod. Only joking, Rob. He's an army doctor who's into fishing and falconry. Me and Dai Young used to start snoring whenever he got on that subject – or we'd hold our hands up in the air and whistle as though we were summoning a budgie. Let's just say he has more sedate interests, but that is the beauty of touring – you get a wide range of characters.

Paul Wallace
Ireland and Saracens
Prop. Age 25
Alias: Wally. Was drafted in as a replacement for Peter Clohessy right at the beginning of the tour and came from nowhere to gain Test selection. He also had a fantastic tour off the field. He's an Irishman, need I say more? I had many hours of fun with him.

Doddie Weir
Scotland & Newcastle
Second row. Age 26
Alias: George (his real name). I nicknamed him Fingers-in-pies, because whatever's going on, he's never far from the pulse. One of the nicest guys you'll ever meet, very witty. His tour was traumatically cut short, which was a huge blow.

Barry Williams
Wales & Neath
Hooker. Age 23
Alias: Barry Four Tours. A young lad who came on tour with just one cap – we called him Four Tours because he spoke as if he'd been on four British Lions tours. Spent many an hour with the doctor and physio in the treatment room deliberating over Test selection. A good player, suited to the style in which we played.

Keith Wood
Ireland & NEC Harlequins
Hooker. Age 25
Alias: The Irish Sperm Whale, or Fester, because he looks like Fester in *The Addams Family*. Shaved head. The judge in the court session. Prolific snorer, to the great annoyance of all his room mates. Unconsciously the most annoying man on tour. Fantastic player.

David Young
Wales & Cardiff
Prop. Age 29
Alias: Dai, or Ted. Hosted a midnight chat show for his room mate every night – he did like a chat at bedtime. Early on he was Jim Telfer's scapegoat. Telf, the forwards coach, would always blame him even when it wasn't his fault.

Nigel Redman

Tony Diprose

Tony Stanger

Fran Cotton

Ian McGeechan

Jim Telfer

Andy Keast

Dave Alred

Dave McLean

Dr James Robson

Mark Davies

Richard Wegrzyk

REPLACEMENTS

Kyran Bracken
England & Saracens
Scrum-half. Age 25
Bit of a pretty boy, smart dresser, good-looking lad. Kyran's one of those rugby players they use to advertise smart suits, like Ben Clarke and Jerry Guscott, not one of the rugged-looking types like me! Only got one opportunity to play and in that game he got injured. He's got the biggest tongue I've ever seen in my life and he shows it as a party trick.

Mike Catt
England & Bath
Fly-half. Age 25
Alias: Catty. A lot of people thought he should have been selected from the start. A gifted footballer. I roomed with him twice – a tremendous room mate who would do anything for his roomy. He is South African, so it was great for him to tour there. He got a bit of stick from the public but it was good-natured and he found that inspirational.

MIKE CATT

Nigel Redman
England & Bath
Lock. Age 32
Alias: Ollie. The sole survivor of my last rugby union international exploit – we were on tour together in Australia in 1988. A very popular call when he got the nod to represent the British Lions and was proud to be made captain. A fantastic ambassador for the sport who gives his all.

Tony Diprose
England & Saracens
No 8. Age 24
Alias: Dippers. Again, came from Argentina. A nice lad who had a good tour and was unfortunate not to play in the final Test.

Tony Stanger
Scotland & Hawick
Scrum-half. Age 29
Good player. He came and played a midweek game for us when Ieuan Evans and Will Greenwood were both hurt and we were struggling with injuries, but he wasn't with us long enough for me to get to know him.

MANAGEMENT

Fran Cotton
Team manager
Got burnt pink by the sun, which was a source of great amusement. The management were obviously a bit older than the players and acted accordingly. They had a lot of socialising to do off the field. But there were times when we all went out for a drink together, and there was a good bond between us. Fran became famous for his quote early in the tour that if you've got any problems with anything at all ... we all expected him to say, 'See me', but wily old Fran said: 'See Stan.' He led by example and was a very proud man.

Ian McGeechan
Head coach
Probably the best coach I've ever worked under in my life. A quietly-spoken man, Geech got the best out of all the players. His coaching techniques were a breath of fresh air. He told me to go out and play rugby and never be scared to try something. He was a very emotive speaker who had me in tears on several occasions in his pre-match speeches. I enjoyed it. My wife complains about me not being emotional, but I found the whole tour very emotional.

Jim Telfer
Assistant coach
A very passionate man. The forwards took a hammering early in the tour and Jim took that very personally. He put the forwards through very long intensive sessions and it paid off in the end. But I used to stand on the training field watching them knock hell out of each other and say, 'Thank God I'm not a forward.' You've never seen a group of guys work so hard. I got on extremely well with him – but then I didn't have to train with him every day.

Andy Keast
Technical coaching assistant
He spent a lot of his time indoors analysing video tapes. As a coach he would have liked to have spent more time on the field. He coached at Natal so it was nice for him to go back to South Africa. Enjoyed himself when given the chance.

Dave Alred
Kicking coach (pictured opposite)
A teetotaller who used to be a professional American footballer for the San Francisco 49ers. It was a luxury to be able to take him, but that shows how professional the tour was. He helped me a lot. He worked hard with Neil Jenkins and Tim Stimpson on their kicking and obvously that bore fruit throughout the tour, but ironically the most famous kick of the tour was the drop goal by Jerry Guscott – and Jerry doesn't work with him.

STAN BAGSHAW

BOB BURROWS

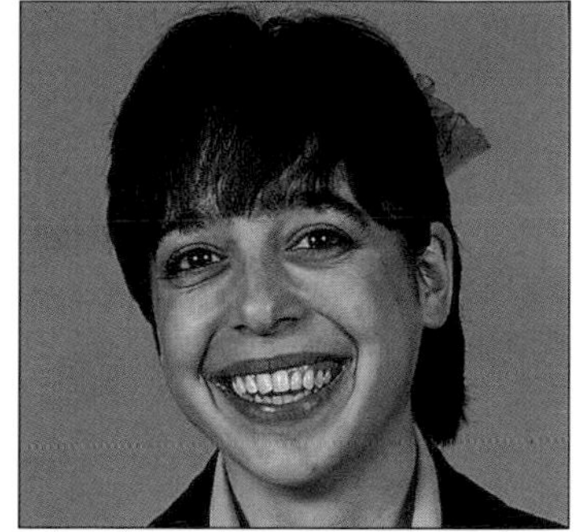

SAMANTHA PETERS

DAVE McLEAN
Fitness adviser
The conditioner. Soccer background. He had a bit of a lonely tour – kept himself to himself. He was in charge of the diet, so he wasn't too popular with some of the boys for not serving up chips and fried eggs and steak every day.

DR JAMES ROBSON
Medical officer
A good doctor and a good friend. I could talk to him about anything and know it would be confidential. He doubled up as a physio, so he spent a lot of time helping Mark Davies, because there were a hell of a lot of niggling bumps and bruises. He had a good tour.

MARK DAVIES
Physiotherapist
I'll be honest, I was disappointed when Kevin Murphy, who had originally been selected as physio, pulled out. But this guy turned out to be one of the stars of the tour. A Welshman who enjoys doing his weights, so to get treatment from him you would have to book it around his gym sessions – he'd be in there with Taity, Dave Young and Scott Gibbs. Nicknamed Carcass, because he loves his body. He lived life to the full.

RICHARD WEGRZYK
Masseur
There were a few eyebrows raised when a masseur was selected, but he was worth his weight in gold. He also practised acupuncture. Mike Catt had it on a regular basis, and Tim Stimpson, Tony Underwood and Richard Hill all used it for stress release.

STAN BAGSHAW
Baggage master
A former rugby league player and a mate of Fran's, it was fantastic for him to tour with the British Lions. He had the unenviable job of getting the baggage properly transported. He also decided who roomed with who, and did of a lot of background organisation. I don't think he ever lost any baggage – it wasn't a case of him losing stuff, the big problem was people unzipping it and taking things out.

DAVE ALRED

BOB BURROWS
Media liaison officer
Battling Bobby Burrows. He got a black eye out on tour and it was jokingly suggested that he got it on some naughty late-night jaunt, but apparently he suffers from a complaint where he bruises easily. But obviously it was the players who were supposed to have the black eyes, not the media man. I helped Bob out a lot. It can be a bit of a chore if things aren't going well, but the way it worked out, his job was not too stressful.

SAM PETERS
Administrative assistant
The Lioness. She worked very hard with all the sponsors, making sure all the branding was right. It's a job that wouldn't have existed a few years ago. These days it's not unusual to see women in a rugby environment – a lot of the lads have female physios at their clubs – but there are not usually women on tour. I'm sure that when Sam took the job she was made fully aware of the trappings of touring with 46 blokes. She's quite open-minded, and she needed to be. The lads didn't go effing and blinding in front of her, but then she swore as much as anybody!

CHAPTER 4

PRE-TOUR DIARY

A squad becomes a team

MONDAY 12 MAY

Gathered at Oatland Park Hotel. Room mate is Jeremy Davidson from Ireland. We are working with a motivating team called IMPACT. Objective is to turn 35 players who have turned up as a squad into a team.

Atmosphere a bit standoffish and everybody a bit tense.

Fitted out with gear from Next and Adidas. There is tons of it.

The tour began when the 35 of us plus 12 management gathered at that hotel in Weybridge. We turned up as a squad and quickly turned ourselves into a team. The management brought in the Impact team – an 11-man motivating team from Windermere who work with professional organisations – and that week was basically spent in teamwork-building activities like absailing and obstacle courses. It was fantastic.

We had to familiarise ourselves very quickly with each other because within a group of 35 guys, initially you've got cliques. The Welsh all stuck together, the lads from Leicester stuck together, the lads from Newcastle stuck together, the lads who had played for England stuck together, the lads who played for Ireland stuck together, and so on. So we had to break those groups down and get everybody working together in a good environment.

It wasn't an attitude that people brought with them. It was one we had to work on.

That was the backbone of the success of the tour, the way we all gelled together, and I can say that during that tour, unlike in any other organisation I've ever experienced, I could go for my breakfast in the morning and the room would be full of guys and I wouldn't look for individuals to sit next to. I could go and sit with anybody.

TUESDAY 13 MAY

Day/tour starts badly. Jeremy and I sleep in and are late for first meeting in Peppercorn Room. Assure management it won't happen again.

Trained at London Irish. Went well. Lads

A squad of Clark Kents – but show these mild-mannered men in blazers a phone box and they turn into wild rugby animals

appreciated my vocal enthusiasm.
Two more Impact sessions.
Long day. Bed late.

We had some very strong characters within the squad. I remember first coming into that room with the other 34 players and thinking that, as far as playing rugby union was concerned, I had very little experience. There were some very, very experienced players there – Ieuan Evans, who had over 70 caps, Martin Johnson ... some lads who had played some very big rugby union. And I had played very little. I could have been intimidated or in awe of these players.

But I deliberately made my presence felt. I'm very vocal and outspoken – I have no problem with communicating with people, whether it be the Lord Mayor or a kid who has just broken into a car. Not everybody is the same, and what I stressed upon all the guys was that it was to the benefit of the side that we all come out of our shells as soon as possible. You can't just buy trust in each other, you've got to develop it and earn respect.

I also realised that touring is unique. It's not just playing rugby union, it's life itself. It's about people dropping barriers and becoming great friends overnight. On tour you eat, sleep and crap with people. It's amazing. A guy that you've only ever seen on the television or played against, you suddenly find yourself rooming with him, following him into the bathroom and things like that. You see a completely different side of a bloke then.

In the past there had been guys who had gone 'off tour'. On the '93 tour there were guys who didn't get selected and then went out on the booze and were a little bit obstructive to what the team was trying to do, and it became a division within the camp. But this was the first professional tour and we were all getting paid. All 35 would get rewarded for the 15 who played in the Test series, so there was no excuse for anybody, if they were disappointed at not being selected, going off tour.

Tour-jackers would not be tolerated. Right at the outset we said there would be disappointments, and massive ones at that. But it was down to the individual how he would handle that.

For instance, of the three hookers, Keith Wood, Barry Williams and Ronnie Reagan, only one could be selected. The other two would be very disappointed. We said it would be a good gesture for the guy who hadn't been selected to go and congratulate the guy who had, because you always feel a bit awkward when you are selected in their place. You don't really like to approach them because it might look like you're being a bit bigger than them. You don't really know how to do it. So to break the ice the guy who hadn't been selected would go and congratulate the other guy.

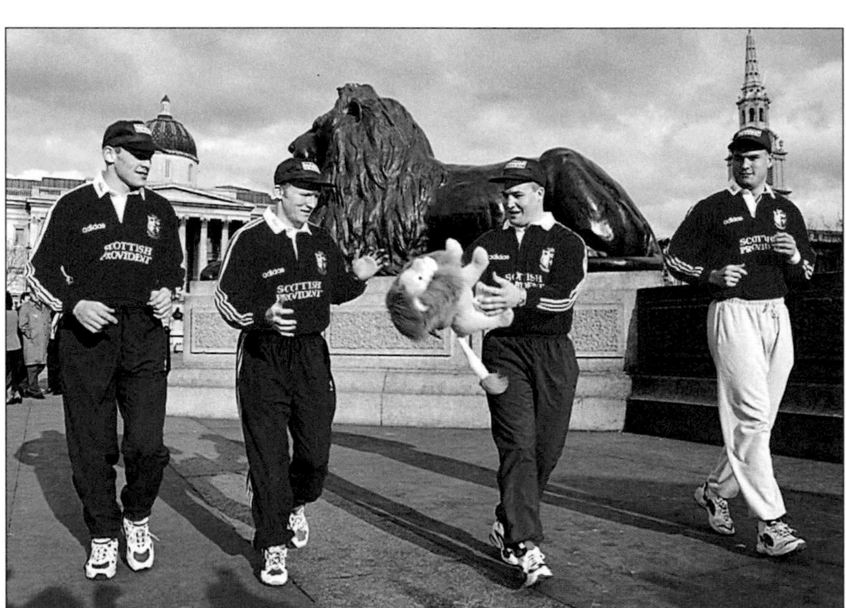

Trafalgar Square Lions: Wainwright, Jenkins, Regan, Davidson in another witty photocall

WEDNESDAY 14 MAY

Big day today. Start with Impact session in canoes on river. Headstands in boat which worry Tim Rodber. We both end up in water after balancing on sides of boat.

Lunch. Training at London Irish. Not as physical as before (shame).

Tea. Change into No.1's. Taity gutted – Next gear doesn't fit. Team photo.

To Café Royal in London for farewell dinner. All split up on individual sponsors' tables. Not as bad as I feared. Jeff Butterfield at dinner but unable to find him.

Missing Sandy and kids despite speaking on phone. Everyone at dinner impressed because nobody drinking. Bed late.

I like it when training is very physical. Early doors, when a group of lads first come together, I enjoy those sessions to try and assert some authority and show the other lads what you're made of – stand up and be counted. Even in professional sport you get lads who don't enjoy training, but I think it's your bread and butter. I could train all day.

The Impact sessions were all about teamwork. A lot of it was peculiar games like building towers of barrels and balancing buckets of water. In that morning's exercise we divided up into groups of eight.

Each group had four two-man canoes side by side and the oarsmen had to swap boats. None of our group had fallen in the water – some of the other lads did, including Fran Cotton. But we made a pact that we would not mess about and we would do it properly. Trouble is, when there's a bit of mischief to be had I'm usually not far away

Captain's log, stardate 1997: 'I am a man alone.' While all the other Lions shared, Martin Johnson had a berth to himself

from it – that's my personality, like it or lump it. You use that to bring the best out of the lads and get them to relax. If people are laughing and joking it's good for team spirit. So I did a headstand on the seat of the canoe. Tim Rodber couldn't believe what I was up to. In the end we both ended up in the water, but it was worth it to see the look on his face.

At the farewell dinner I was sat at a table with a nice group of guys from a computer firm in London. I spent the evening as their guest, which is always difficult. Ideally you want to sit with your mates and make easy conversation and it doesn't matter if you break wind at the table or slurp your drink. But we were on show for the evening. People were there to see us and give us a good sending-off. I was just sorry I couldn't track down Jeff Butterfield, because he's not only a Lions legend, he also comes from my home town, Cleckheaton.

There were many other Lions of the past there, and meeting them brought home how massive the task in hand was going to be. Gerald Davies spoke at the dinner, and he gave us a motto we used throughout the coming weeks: Whingeing is the constant companion of losers.

On the tour things didn't go right all the time, but it was at those times that I remembered the words of Gerald Davies. We eradicated moaning from our lives.

'What's that, Ieuan?' 'I think it's one of those new-fangled camera thingies, Jerry.' Elderly Lions prepare for their third tour

THURSDAY 15 MAY

Still more gear coming our way. Impact sessions plus video input by Andy Keast.

People getting on well. No bad individuals. Atmosphere good.

Press conference and team photo in kit. Press interest is massive. Like nothing experienced before. Learned that press will be in our hotel – be careful!

Initially there were a few eyebrows raised when we were told that the press would be staying in the same hotel as us throughout the tour. It sets alarm bells ringing because you have to behave. You tend to feel that the notepad is never away.

As it turned out, they were very good – but then the tour was a success and that helped them sell newspapers. Fran's not daft. He said you'll never beat the press, we need the press on our side, so it was a shrewd move. But if we had been losing every game we would have been dodging them all the time.

As far as staying out at night and so on was concerned, they were worse than us. They had a good tour!

ANDY KEAST was our video wizz. After every match he did an individual tape for every player. The computer equipment can take every moment that a player is involved during 80 minutes and compress it into a four-minute video – tackling, running with the ball, support play, everything.

I watch videos of myself before every game at Halifax and at Newcastle as part of my preparation. We all like to watch ourselves play well on tape, but I also like to watch when I've had

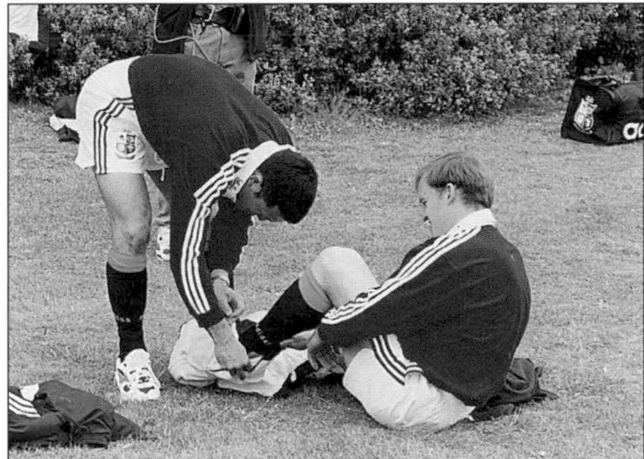

Lions in training, clockwise from top left: Rob Wainwright concentrates as Ian McGeechan spouts; Jeremy Guscott does a runner; Tony Underwood shows Gregor Townsend how to tie up his laces; Will Greenwood has a ball with the superglue

a poor game. I usually like to do it in private, because the camera never lies. There are moments that make you wince, like the Joubert tackle in the Second Test. I missed that tackle, and he went on to score – and of course I had the opportunity to see it many times with all the other players and it was a source of great embarrassment.

But one thing about getting older and more experienced is that if I make a mistake I realise it immediately. When you are younger you dwell on it, but you need to put it to the back of your mind.

In team talks I always say that players *will* make mistakes. It's not the fact that you've made a mistake, what's more important is the manner in which you recover. The last thing a player needs when he has made a mistake is his team-mates getting on him and bollocking him. One thing we worked on with the Lions is that if anyone makes a mistake, we should consciously make an effort to pat him on the back and gee him up, and make an extra effort not to allow them to score – because that's the worse that can happen. With great team spirit and enthusiasm in defence, we were able to do that.

It's easy for me to talk about scoring the 'Try of the Tour', but at the same time I've got to be able to talk about the missed tackle. I remember wanting a shovel to dig a big hole and climb into because there were 60,000 people watching and laughing. You get behind the posts and you can see it in the faces of the other lads: you know you've let the team down.

It's a big inner fight then, and you've got to respond in a positive manner. The best thing you can do is get the ball in your hands as quickly as possible, or make an effective tackle and get back into the game and eradicate that mistake.

It's not just about playing rugby, it's about life. If somebody has confidence, it's hard to put them down.

FRIDAY 16 MAY

Training at London Irish. Return to hotel where sign hundreds of shirts/balls.

Big Impact session.

Asked to do summing up speech, which went well. Camera crew with us throughout for documentary. Dinner.

Stan Bagshaw (the man) sorts local pub out and we all go for compulsory drink. Free beer – brilliant. Great night. People really come out of their shells. As important/as much gained as Impact sessions. To bed 4am – tired/drunk.

One of the guys from Impact had asked me if I would present our group's team talk to the whole squad. This was the first of my many speeches throughout the tour – they started calling me Winston. I only speak from the heart. It was about team spirit and how we wouldn't allow tour-jackers and we had to be responsible for each other. The eyes of the world are upon us. We're going out there and nobody gives us a chance and if we want it we'll get it.

We had roughed out the speech together as a group using flip charts, but then I got up there and went into my Winston Churchill mode, and the lads took the piss.

Usually with touring teams the three B's are pretty prevalent. That's the birds, the booze and the brawling. But we hadn't had a drink all week. So on the Friday night we all went out to a local pub in Weybridge and had a good drink together, which I firmly believe is a vital ingredient in team spirit and bonding. It was a fantastic evening. Of course, you see another side of a bloke when he's got a few beers in him. People drop their inhibitions. It was good. Next morning everybody woke up with sore heads.

SATURDAY 17 MAY

Full breakfast – the works. Spend all morning staring at kit spread around bedroom hoping it will pack itself.

Watch FA Cup Final whilst packing. Chelsea 2 Middlesbrough 0.

Barbecue in afternoon for lads and local wives. Too far for Sandy and children.

Into No.1's. Selected as entertainment manager.

Depart hotel at 7pm to Heathrow airport. Made very welcome. First class flight: 10pm leave UK. Massage proves popular with all lads on flight. To sleep.

Being entertainments manager was quite an important role, as it turned out, but I was reluctant to take it because when I went to Australia in '88 I was remembered for the things I did off the field, not the things I did on it – the drinking and carrying on and that sort of thing. This time I was hoping not to be part of that, if I was strong enough.

We had a players' meeting and we said there's going to be plenty of spare time on the tour, we can't just play and train, so we need to select someone as entertainments manager. Well, about 10 people in the room shouted my name out straight away.

So eventually I said, 'All right, I'll do it, but I want to pick my own people to help me.' The first person I thought of was Jerry Guscott because Jerry's very outspoken and if he doesn't want to do something, he doesn't do it. He can be very cutting and quite intimidating. I didn't want him on my

LIONS LAWS 1997

THE FOLLOWING BEHAVIOURS ARE ESSENTIAL FOR SUCCESS:

Winners	Cohesive	Trust
Highest standards	Supportive	United
Discipline (self & team)	Openness	Committed
Desire	Honesty	Flexible
Dedication	Enjoyment	Punctual
Belief (self & others)	Positive	No cliques
Identity	Constructive	Respect personal space

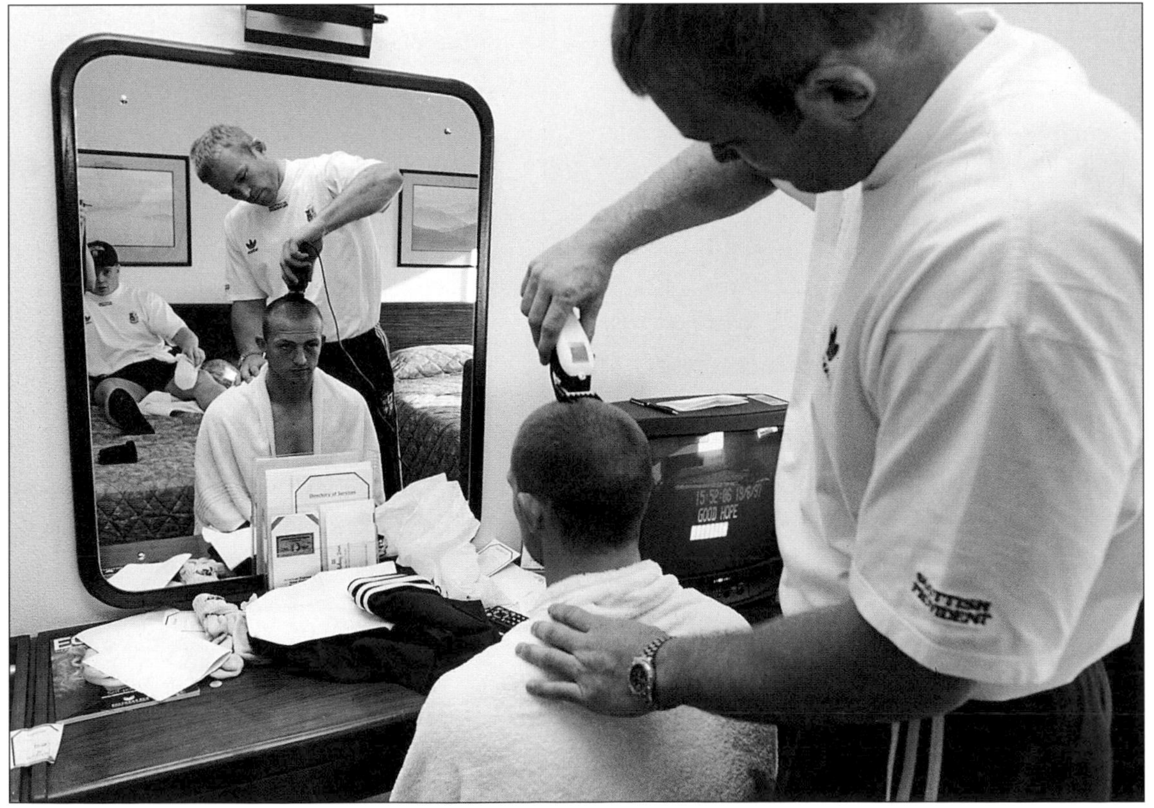

'Bin on holiday yet? Nice weather? See EastEnders last night?' Hairdresser Tim Rodber gives Matt Dawson a close shave

The British and Irish Lions touring party. Back, from left: Allan Bateman, Mark Regan, Rob Howley, Neil Jenkins, Barry Williams, Paul Grayson, Nick Beal, Tim Stimpson, John Bentley, Tom Smith, Gregor Townsend, Paul Wallace, Neil Back, Austin Healey, Andy Keast. Middle: Stan Bagshaw, Alan Tait, Keith Wood, Eric Miller, Scott Quinnell, Will Greenwood, Jeremy Davidson, Simon Shaw, Doddie Weir, Tim Rodber, Lawrence Dallaglio, Richard Hill, Graham Rowntree, Matt Dawson, Dave McLean, Bob Burrows, Richard Wegrzyk. Front: Sam Peters, Dr James Robson, Jason Leonard, David Young, Ieuan Evans, Mark Davies, Fran Cotton, Martin Johnson, Ian McGeechan, Jim Telfer, Jeremy Guscott, Rob Wainwright, Tony Underwood, Scott Gibbs, Dave Alred

back for eight weeks chipping away at me, so the first thing I did the next day was get him on my side. He came on along with Doddie Weir and Scott Gibbs.

Everywhere we went we met with the local liaison officers and with Jonty Goslett of the South African rugby union and decided what to put on during the players' free time. Golf, snorkelling, videos – these little things are important, because if they're not there you get lads whining. Every Thursday we would all go out for a meal together, and we decided where to go. Obviously golf was the most popular activity, but go-karting was popular, and very competitive. In Johannesburg

we jacked up a shark board – the lads went and dissected a shark and had their photos taken. In Durban the lads went in the surf on jet skis. We had a team room with a table tennis table, pool table, darts board, video, and a constant supply of fruit and drinks – mainly non-alcoholic. There was alcohol as well but you wouldn't find anyone drinking 72 hours before a game.

THE MOOD at the end of the first week was very different from at the beginning. Before I arrived in Weybridge I thought it was great to be on the tour, but I didn't know if we could beat the world champions. We were real long-shots. We didn't have the individuals of the '74 Lions. The best I thought we could do was compete in the Tests.

We all got a payment for being on tour. We also got a payment for being well behaved on tour – a bonus which nobody lost, by the way. There was a payment for winning one Test and a payment for winning the series. I remember speaking to my wife, Sandy – and I'm sure many others did – and I told her not to account for that money. In my heart of hearts I didn't think we could win the series.

But I can honestly say that by the end of that week in Weybridge, by the time we left Heathrow and flew to Johannesburg, all 47 of us firmly believed that we were going to win.

CHAPTER 5

TOUR DIARY • WEEK 1

Welcome to the Rainbow Nation

SUNDAY 18 MAY

1000 hrs arrive Johannesburg. Big tedious press conference. All lads are tired.

1400 hours dep Johannesburg to Durban. Book into Beverly Hills Hotel after welcome by tribesmen. Rooming with Dai Young, Welsh prop.

Select entertainment committee. Doddie Weir, Scott Gibbs, Stan Bagshaw, Jeremy Guscott. Must get him on my side – could be a problem otherwise with moaning/ criticising.

All lads relax in hotel. Evening meal. Good chat with Barry Williams, Alan Tait, Dai Young.

Bedtime. Thought I could talk – Youngey won't shut his mouth.

The press conference in Johannesburg was hard work. It's not ideal the minute you land in a foreign country after a long flight. We had got on the plane in No.1's – our blazers and ties – then changed into leisure gear. But then we had to get back into our No.1's, all feeling a bit fusty, and get off the plane to do the press conference. Then we had to get on another plane and fly on to Durban!

We were glad to get there. We had 11 moves during the tour and the policy was that at each hotel you would room with a different person. You wouldn't room with anyone from your own country, which was quite easy do do because initially there were 18 Englishmen and 17 others. Martin Johnson, the captain, roomed on his own, so there were 17 and 17. Wherever possible, the lads who were playing in the Test matches roomed together – that was common sense, because the other lads could then go out and have a beer.

Rooming with someone can make or break a friendship. You see all kinds of peculiar things. I'm quite neat and tidy and I tell you it's damned annoying when you get somebody who has a shave and doesn't swill out the sink, or someone like Alan Tait who has a wee and doesn't flush it. You

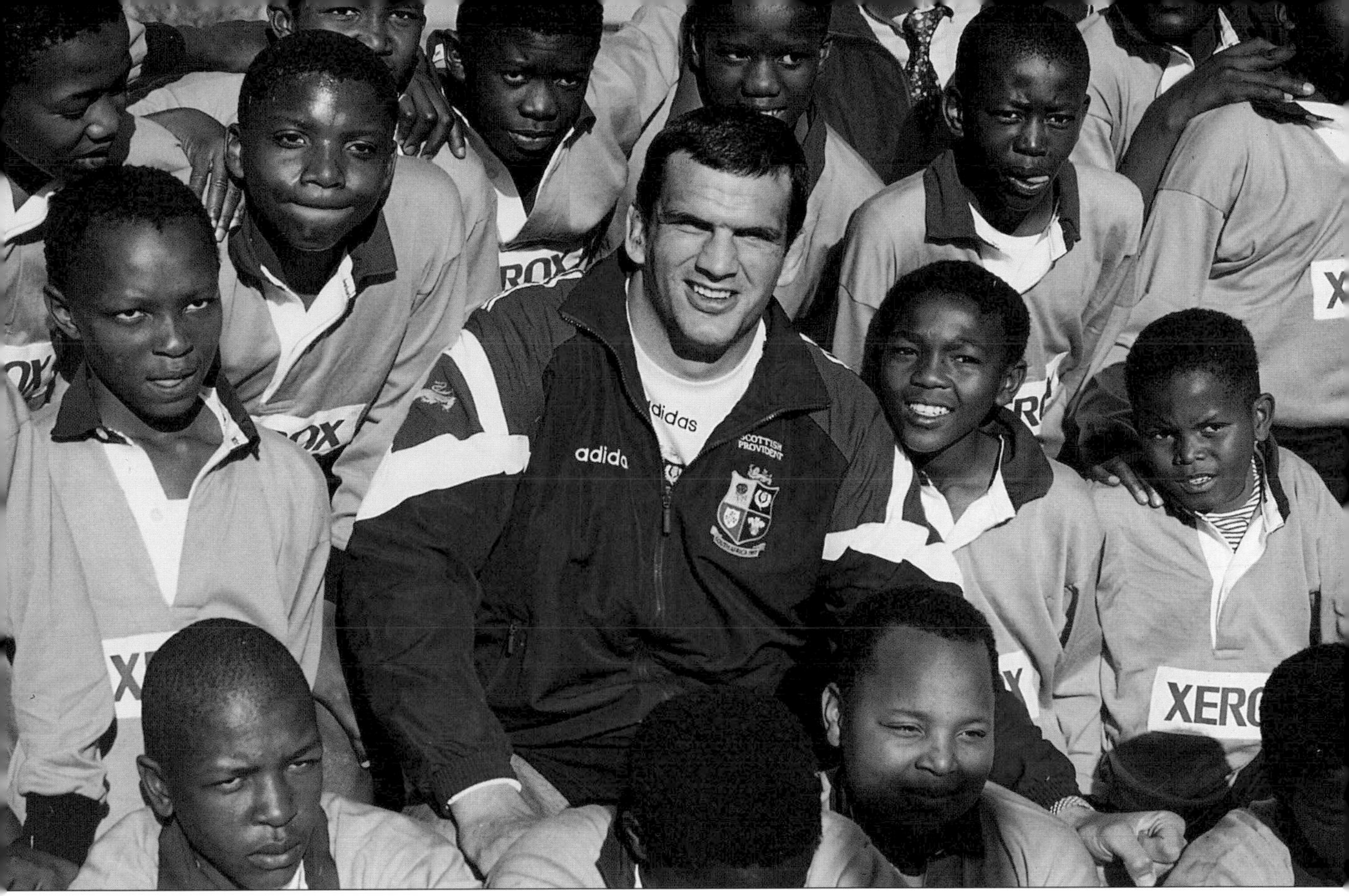

'Everywhere we went everybody waved, everybody smiled.' Martin Johnson enjoys the warmth of South African hospitality

get some lads who are very untidy and some who are very neat; you get some who like to talk a lot and some who don't; some who are getting homesick, some who have got families, some who haven't; some young lads touring for the first time, some who've been on tour many times...

You've got to be pretty considerate. There are times when your room mate wants to be on his own. Sometimes when you've had a beer, you come in late and your mate's already in bed preparing for a game. I understand that on a couple of occasions that led to heated words being spoken.

Earplugs in, it's Keith Wood – the Lions' notorious snorer

The longest stretch we had with one person was 11 days in Pretoria and I spent those 11 days with Keith Wood. We obviously gave each other plenty of respect. The only problem with Keith is that he's a shocking snorer. He's notorious for it. You have to put the old earplugs in or have a glass of water ready to throw at him, which I did on a couple of occasions.

But it was fantastic to room with different people and get to know them a little bit closer. I couldn't help seeing a letter that one of my room mates wrote to his girlfriend. It was a bit cheeky really, but I read it ... and he does some peculiar things to his girlfriend. I didn't dare mention it for two or three days. He was a bit annoyed with me, as you might expect, but you know what it's like when you skim through a book and one word jumps out at you and all of a sudden you're in a sex scene. This word just jumped out of the page. I couldn't believe it. But he forgave me.

My first room mate, Dai Young, is a good lad – we played rugby league together at Leeds. We got on well. No snoring, no sex scenes, and no bristles in the sink. But he does like a chat at night...

MONDAY 19 MAY

Breakfast – team meeting. Training outside Natal Sharks' King's Park. Looks impressive stadium. Lots of contact with forwards. Good bashing with Gibbsy.

Return to hotel where fax waiting. Donald Ross again bringing tear to the eye with good luck wishes from all at Cleckheaton club. 'ALWAYS REMEMBER YOUR ROOTS.' Must do well for them/& me.

Video shop sorted so we get 2 different videos per day for lads to watch.

Dai Young doesn't stop chattering at bedtime.

Me and Gibbsy in Durban. Bit of a shock. People/women/children sleeping on streets. Sad place.

Jonty Goslett, the SARFU rep, took Scott Gibbs and me into Durban for a look around. It was a bit of an eye-opener. There were so many poor people on the streets. We saw a mother with a very, very young child who was obviously sleeping on the street. We got the VIP treatment everywhere we went and it was a shocking contrast. But you have to pull yourself away from it. You have to remain focused.

The profile of rugby union in South Africa is unbelievable – I've never experienced anything like it. At every hotel we had a fantastic reception, with Zulu dancers to greet us and wonderful hospitality. Even driving around in our bus, although the bus wasn't plastered with the words 'British Lions', everybody recognised us. And everybody waved, everybody smiled, everybody pointed, everybody stopped what they were doing as we went past.

It wasn't like travelling around England. Nobody stuck two fingers up at us or gave us an ill-mannered gesture. I've turned up at Coventry with Newcastle and the coach got spat on. In South Africa, the hospitality was fantastic. It was a different kettle of fish when we got on the field...

THE TRAINING was becoming hard work now. Some of the training sessions were harder than some of the games and you had to be mentally right for them. It's not easy to go in full out against your mates, but if you go in half-hearted, that's when you get hurt. There were a lot of injuries in training, nothing serious fortunately, but lads with cut eyes and cuts on their heads, strains and pulls.

On the training field the backs and forwards worked separately, practising their set pieces. The forwards would practise lineouts and scrummaging techniques while we would work on our defensive alignment and our play from scrums, general plays and moves and familiarisation with each other. But when we played the contact stuff we intermingled and split into two groups of 16 and knocked seven bells out of each other.

The training was all planned and programmed to what lay ahead. Early on in the tour we were knocking the stuffing out of each other in an effort to provide realistic opposition. It's no use practising all these fancy moves that you like to do without the obstacles that you get put in front of you on a match day. Anybody can run through an unopposed session and put together all the fancy handling things. But the time that you get smacked by a 16-stone guy is the time that you find out whether you can get the ball away or not, or

That's one way to put some bite into their play: Scott Gibbs and Rob Howley take time off in Durban to visit a 'shark board'

whether you have to hold on and react accordingly.

You know the golden old saying, you only get out what you put in. We put a hell of a lot of work in. It was very competitive because there were 15 Test spots up for grabs and eight matches to play before the Test matches. Everybody saw it as an opportunity to shine in training – both by the manner in which you trained and the way you played against your opposite number.

You can't be training like that the day before the game, but one thing we stressed was that we needed to train with the intensity of a match environment, so as to be honest with each other.

TUESDAY 20 MAY

Training session in morning. Paul Grayson trains for full session. Still intense with plenty of contact.

Press conference at hotel. Talk about 1988 tour entertainment/alcohol code of conduct/discipline. Duncan on camera crew gives me handycam to use. To gym where use handycam.

7.00pm meeting with Geech in his room on backs moves/defence.

Presented with ghettoblaster by Susan Sneddon from Scottish Provident.

Bus dep 2100 hrs, optional night out to Thirsty's in Durban Harbour then on to TJ's. Head man Chris, doorman Freddie. Top night. Full of it. Bus leaves midnight. Not everyone on it. Every jack for himself.

Drinks are so cheap. 4 Castle lagers, two Bacardi and cokes 30 Rand – £4.25. Full night out, that's all I spent.

Things were amazingly cheap over there. That night when I went to the bar, the lad from Adidas, Hugh, asked me to get his beers in because the bar was busy, and I paid about 49 rand for his round and mine. He spent ages trying to work out how much he owed me and eventually realised we were arguing the toss about £3.50. We just burst out laughing.

Quite a few of the lads bought diamonds in Cape Town. I bought Sandy an eternity ring with four diamonds set in it, and I got my two daughters a loose diamond each to make into a ring when they are 18. I also brought home a krugerrand gold coin for my son.

WEDNESDAY 21 MAY

BRILLIANT NEWS. Selected in team on r/wing for 1st game on Saturday. Big boost to tour, which is going well.

Trained – physical with contact. Hurt R shin/toe when Austin Healey tackled. No great problem. Tim Stimpson and Tim Rodber both down with stomach bug. Confined to rooms.

Interview by press in afternoon plus TV show. Boys visit Shark Board and go on beach or just relax. I have treatment for injury to my right big toe.

Had backs moves written down by Gregor Townsend.

Sent letter home to Sandy

1997 Lions laws finalised & handed out to players.

As fly-half, Gregor Townsend is the one who calls the moves, so I asked him to write them down for me. We've all probably done most of them before, but they've got different names. We had moves called Scotland, World Class, ACT, Raiders. Nothing logical, just whatever he comes up with. But we all had a big input into what the moves actually were.

Running the angles is the big thing in rugby these days, and it's a style that comes from rugby league. We play it at Newcastle, where the other rugby league guys and I have had a big influence. On the Lions tour it was new to some of the guys from other clubs.

If the player with the ball runs diagonally across the field and all his team mates move with him, the defence can just move across to pick them all off. So you have to offer the guy with the ball different options. The people who do the hard work are the guys off the ball who come at angles opposite to the runner with the ball. So you come under him and give him the option of a drop or a scissors. We worked a lot of those: the dummy scissors pop, the dummy scissors miss, the drift ball.

WHAT YOU'RE basically doing in back play is trying to create a disorganised defence out of an organised defence. When you start from a scrum or a lineout it's an organised defence, man on man. To create a disorganised defence the people without the ball in their hands have to do specific things.

If you get a bloke running across the field with the ball in his hand and you've got two blokes waiting for a pass outside him, it may be that one of those has to unselfishly come inside him on a different angle to 'stand up' the defence – i.e., to make at least one of their running defenders stop, stand up and maybe have to go the other way. Once the defender loses momentum he's less of a threat. The man running at the angle may receive the ball, he may not. Sometimes you would run as a decoy runner just to try and open a gap somewhere.

The key is identifying what the ball-carrier expects of the people around him, and you do that by developing a familiarity with each other and by being consistent in the way you play. We have set-piece calls, whether it be an intricate move that would involve players running different lines, players getting dropped off on scissors, or whether

The first training session in South Africa: Ian McGeechan formulates the tactics that will bring down the world champions

it be more straightforward, like one player – Scott Gibbs or myself for instance – running to link up with our back row to tie their back row in and then move the play somewhere else.

Ian McGeechan, the Lions coach, recognised that you can only premeditate so much. You can only call the first move. If you say, for instance, that the centre is going to hit it up from the fly-half and tie the back row in, we may tie two of their centres in. We may not tie any of them in. You then have to adapt to what's in front of you: you can't possibly plan it all the way through.

So you have this array of moves but a lot of them you may not use. It all depends on what's in front of you. Basically, if they've got an extra man in their defence, you've got to do something to tie that extra man in. It's no use trying to push it wide because they are just going to have numbers on you. Whereas if they've got one man less, you've got to try to tie them in and release your end man. It can become a bit of a game of chess. That was how we played it. It's important to remember that as soon as you get the ball you're not necessarily trying to score, you have to maintain possession.

IT'S HARD for a side to defend for long periods. Geech calculated that there were times when we were defending for 90 seconds. That is a hell of a thing to ask, continuous defending. We identified that if we could keep possession for 90 seconds, it would be nigh on impossible to stop us scoring.

It takes confidence and patience to slip an arm or half a tackle and not to give a fifty-fifty pass, but to hold on to the ball, get men behind the ball and recycle it, and shift them somewhere else and continue to do that. At some point a mistake in their defence will hopefully allow us to score.

You use certain players for certain skills. We would use Scott Gibbs or myself as a battering ram to try and get over the advantage line and lay the ball back. You don't use Jeremy Guscott like that.

You saw more of that battering-ram style on this tour because of the way we were allowed to play by the referees, who let us hold the ball while on the ground, which Northern Hemisphere referees would penalise.

That was a massive factor in our approach. I could go into a gang tackle, two or three players, and be 99 per cent confident that the ball would come back, because I could hold the ball while lying on the floor. Our players would be very close and come over the top and their players would be instructed to leave the ball alone. At that point I could release the ball and push it back.

There were two ways of dissuading defenders from putting their hands on the ball. Either they would be penalised – and with a kicker like Neil Jenkins, that is points on the board – or they would get their hand kicked off ... and deservedly so.

The games were very physical. I remember on a couple of occasions getting in front of the ball and not being able to get away and I got a right kicking. It's at times like that that a back finds out how it feels to be a forward. Some of those boys get their backs ripped up, bruises and grazes all down their legs that stay there for the remainder of the tour, and they never even mention it. I get a little scratch on my leg and I get the ointment out.

THURSDAY 22 MAY

Had to miss training because of bruising to big toe. Whilst session running, me, Ted [David Young], Taity, Bateman, Gibbs all nursing injuries. So much for hard men from league. Good session by lads. Ieuan filled in for me.

Free afternoon. To Langoustines seafood restaurant in evening after having hair cut in hotel.

After what I've been saying about the influence of the hardened 'super-professional' rugby league guys, it was a source of great amusement to the union lads to see David Young, Alan Tait, Allan Bateman, Scott Gibbs and me all sitting it out. One of the lads took a photo and they all had a good laugh at us. I made myself feel better by having a haircut – the first of about four during the trip.

FRIDAY 23 MAY

Richard Hill's birthday. Trained. Concerned about toe. May have to pull out.

12.30pm. Disappointment. Pulled out of game. Still a long way to go. Don't want to mess things up. Ieuan Evans steps in.

Hilda's birthday. Interrupt press conference and present him cake. Thrown in pool. Wally [Paul Wallace] also pushed in by Ronnie Regan. Relax.

Leave hotel 4pm. 1 hr flight to Port Elizabeth. 5 mins to Holiday Inn. Nice hotel – big beds, fast lifts. Rooming with Gregor Townsend.

Meal was very poor lamb-type curry. Also some of baggage failed to arrive. Management not happy but must stay focused. Dai Young taking piss out of spot on Stimo's nose. Plus Jim Telfer still having a go at him.

Treatment. Reflexology.

By now this toe injury was beginning to be a problem. It had happened on Wednesday when I got tackled by Austin Healey and I knocked my toe back. People laugh about big toe injuries, but two doctors felt that it was fractured. I had had to pull out the first game – and it was suggested to me that if I didn't train on Sunday and play in the next game I would be sent home.

It continued to cause me grief throughout the tour even though I had constant treatment on it. It didn't affect me when I was running, but it gave me stick when I was in bed – it was almost as annoying as Keith Wood's snoring.

Doddie's Holiday Snaps

It's 5 am and the boys have beaten the Germans to the sun beds...

We were sharing the hotel with the Supremes convention.

'Do you think the management will twig these are our wives and girlfriends?'

After two hours, Fran gave the boys a ball to play with.

'Sorry, these two chairs are for Simon Shaw.'

'What are you hiding behind the flag, Doddie?' 'My helmet.'

MATCH REPORT

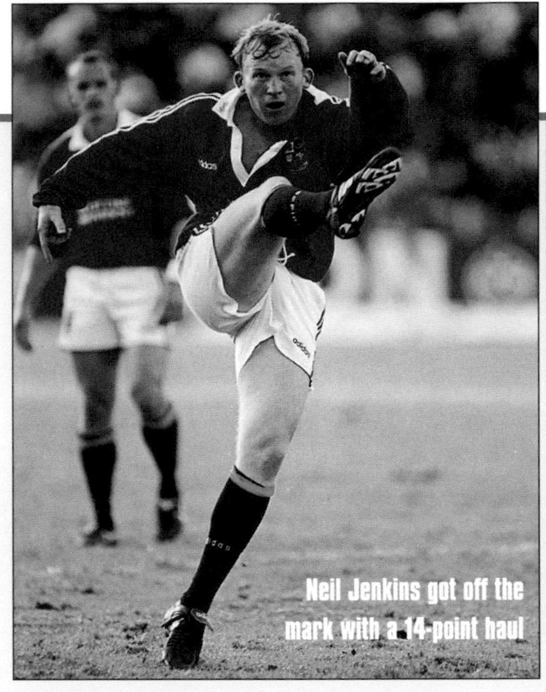

Neil Jenkins got off the mark with a 14-point haul

EASTERN PROVINCE 11 LIONS 39

Port Elizabeth, May 24

THE LIONS tour got off to a wobbly start with a flattering scoreline against one of South Africa's weakest provincial sides. Until Eastern Province wilted towards the end, the Lions looked clumsy and uncoordinated, and at 10-11 down were in danger of losing.

It had all started so promisingly with a scorching try by Jeremy Guscott after good work by virtually the entire Lions team. But with Springbok star Kobus Wiese reinforcing the big Eastern Province pack, the Lions forwards could not win sufficient possession.

The backs had been spilling the ball and missing their touch kicks, but they came to the rescue with a blitz of late tries. Guscott and Will Greenwood both looked sharp and Neil Jenkins' kicking boot was working well.

EASTERN PROVINCE – Try: Kayser. Pens: Van Rensburg 2.

LIONS – Tries: Guscott 2, Weir, Underwood, Greenwood. Cons: Jenkins 4. Pens: Jenkins 2.

EASTERN PROVINCE: T Van Rensburg, D Kayser, R van Jaarsveld, H le Roux (R Loubscher 80), H Pedro, K Ford (R Fourie 43), C Alcock, D Saayman, J Kirsten (capt) (M Winter 80), W Enslin (W Lessing 40), M Webber, J Wiese, S du Preez, S Scott-Young, J Greeff.

LIONS: N Jenkins, I Evans (T Underwood 68), J Guscott, W Greenwood, N Beal, G Townsend, R Howley, T Smith, K Wood (B Williams 68), J Leonard, G Weir, S Shaw (J Davidson 74), L Dallaglio, R Hill, S Quinnell.

'Thirty-nine points was very encouraging. I was delighted at the way we finished the game, regaining the control we had shown in the first 20 minutes. But we did lose control in the middle period.' – *IAN McGEECHAN, Lions coach*

'The Lions look vulnerable playing backwards.' – *JOHAN KLUYTS, Eastern Province coach*

'They can definitely be taken up front.' – *JACO KIRSTEN, Eastern Province captain*

SATURDAY 24 MAY

Match day. 1st game, v Eastern Prov Inv XV. Team in good mood. Morning free for boys to do as they choose.

I have treatment with Carcass (physio) then go for walk along beach with him.

Assist Gregor in preparing for game. Depart for game. Usual routine.

Big crowd there. Game won 39-11.

Male streaker beaten up on top of train at top of terracing by bouncer. Bouncer turned on by angry crowd.

'I was pleased with how the game went for me. The mistakes we made were mostly those of a side who hadn't played together before.' – *JEREMY GUSCOTT*

Reception/speeches. Return to hotel where have drink then change and then go out together for meal. Food takes ages though enjoyable. Watch England beat South Africa 2-1 at soccer.

Return to hotel to pack. Can't go out cos haven't played. Must be growing up. All lads out. Bed. Must get fit.

The incident with the streaker was really upsetting. At the top part of the stadium on the far side from the main stand, there was a train – an engine with four or five carriages behind it – that had been turned into a bar and restaurant. A guy got on the roof and took all his clothes off and was streaking across the top of it. One of the bouncers got up and absolutely knocked the shit out of him, sickeningly. The game was going on, but everybody was watching this. He got him by the hair and bashed his head. Well, the crowd turned on this bouncer and chased him off and eventually he got beaten up badly and tied to a fence.

I was proud of myself for staying in that night. I made a conscious decision not to go out, whereas in 1988 I probably would have done. I decided that my time will come on tour, but I have to get my foot right. Once I'm fit to play I can start enjoying myself.

CHAPTER 6

TOUR DIARY • WEEK 2

A Small altercation

SUNDAY 25 MAY

Good day. Trained fully. Picked in team to play on Wednesday against Border. Fantastic.

Packed and left PE. Flew to East London. Got on coach on runway, which then broke down outside airport. Didn't have to wait long for spare bus.

Rooming with Ieuan Evans. Sorted pictures out for lads. Me, Leonard, Wood, Guscott walked to club The Revue Bar only to find it shut on Sundays.

I wasn't popular, since it said that in booklet on advert.

Sent postcards home.

This club was down on the sea front and, between you and me, it was a strip joint. Jerry and I decided that in our capacity as the entertainment committee, we ought to check it out. Unfortunately it was closed. The lads weren't too pleased.

MONDAY 26 MAY

Breakfast. Treatment. Toe flared up slightly. Trained as team, full contact.

Back to hotel where relax using handycam. Climbed balcony and broke into bathroom where caught X wanking.

Interviews w Chris Jones, Stuart Barnes.

Devastated – Realised X had snook up into my room and wiped out the video evidence.

Rang home in evening at 6pm. Spoke to Faye who sounded very down. Not usual self. She sounded upset. Spoke to Lloyd & Sandy. God I miss them all. Millie struggling with nappies/teeth. Faye too upset & crying to come back on phone. My mind was on that. Upset me. Watched 2 videos. Bed.

Faye is my eldest daughter – she's five. We are very close. She was obviously upset and when you are on the other side of the world and are not due home for six weeks, it isn't very nice.

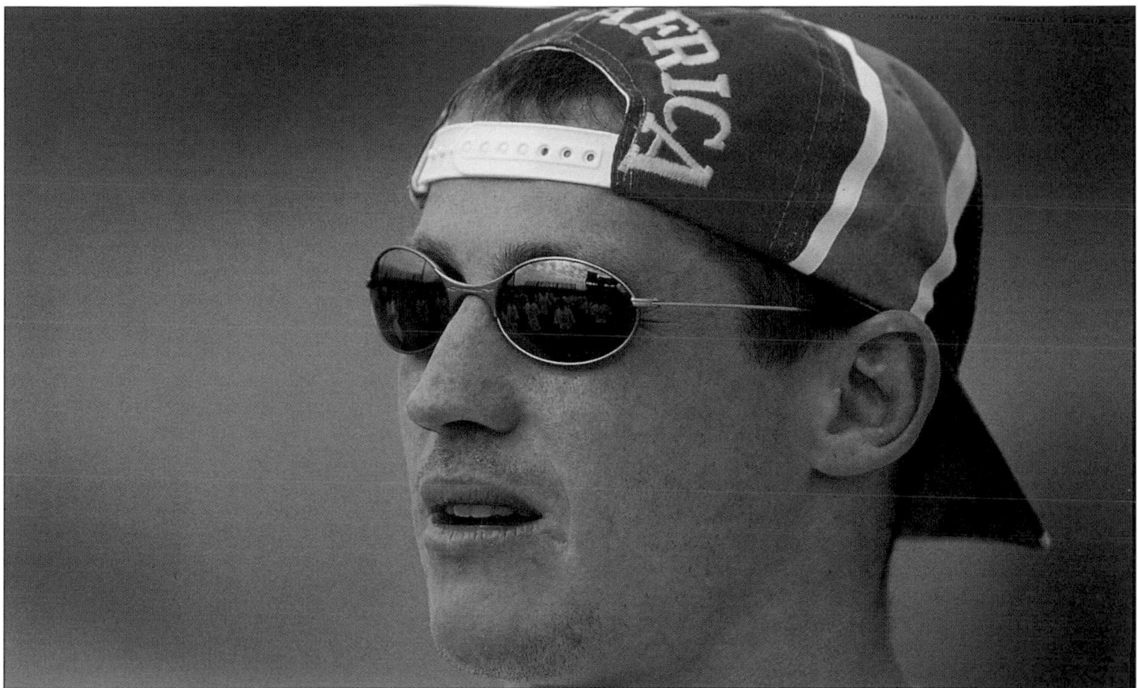

On the lookout for Mr Bentley: James Small, hero and villain of South African rugby – and their most-capped player

Earlier, there had been fisticuffs on the training field between Mark Regan and Barry Williams. The two hookers lost their rag after a clash of heads in the scrum. Coach Jim Telfer had to pull them apart, but it is a sign of how committed everyone is. As Fran Cotton told the press: 'If you are going to be tough on the opposition, you have to be tough on yourselves first.'

The best laugh of the day came when I caught a team mate on camera in a case of self-abuse. The film crew who were making the tour documentary had paid a substantial amount of money to get access to us. But early doors, whenever the camera went on, the lads reacted accordingly. So the crew gave me a tiny hand-held camera. I didn't shout my mouth off saying I'd got it from them, but I didn't trick anybody ... except this once. I'd been asked to get the lads behaving normally, and that's what he was doing. Anyway, he managed to destroy the evidence – but I had already shown a dozen of the lads so it wasn't a problem.

TUESDAY 27 MAY

Mum's birthday. Rang home to wish her happy birthday.

Team training session. Bad weather – Raining.

Free afternoon. First afternoon sleep. Lads go-karting/videos.

Team meeting. Relax.

So here I was looking forward to my first game at last – playing for the midweek team. On previous Lions tours, that would have been a strong indication that you were not going to play in the Tests. The midweek guys were very much the reserves. But that was a vital factor in this tour – we were all determined that the midweek team should not be seen as second best.

The selectors are only human and obviously before leaving these shores they had a team in mind for the first Test. But due to the form of the side that played midweek, that selection was turned on its head. What became very apparent was that there were 35 players in contention for Test spots, not just 15 players and six subs.

The boys who weren't playing also had a big role to play. For instance, if we were preparing for a game on the Saturday, the guys who weren't playing had to provide very intense and formidable opposition for the guys in training – which we all did.

Here's a measure of the team spirit. Throughout the tour the team who had played got the next day off to rehabilitate and take it easy. After we won the First Test the lads who had played had a big night out drinking, but in the team room the next morning they announced that they would train fully that day and provide stiff opposition for the guys who were due to play midweek

It was a fantastic gesture. They didn't have to train. It would have been quite easy for them to lounge around the pool. But it was very much a united front.

I played both midweek and Saturday games, but where I made a bit of a name for myself was playing midweek. The best rugby we played on tour was midweek against the likes of Gauteng, Northern Transvaal and Emerging Springboks.

In the past the midweek team had been known as the dirt-trackers. Well, I objected to that. A TV interviewer referred to me as a dirt-tracker and I stopped him in his tracks. I said: 'I'm not a dirt-tracker – I'm a player here playing for a Test place along with the 14 others who played today.' There was no division between the Test side and the midweek side. We didn't have any dirt-trackers.

WEDNESDAY 28 MAY

MATCH DAY. LIONS –v– BORDER.

I. Evans up early & training. Laze in bed. 1000 Breakfast with Scott Gibbs.

No studs for boots yet.

1100 Team meeting.

Light run with backs. Studs arrive.

1130 Beans on toast. Nervous – which is good.

1515. Kick off. Field waterlogged. 2 -3 inches of water on pitch. Score try with 1st touch of ball. Have good game. Win 18-14.

Scott Gibbs injured. Transpired damaged ankle ligaments. 7 to 10 days out. Relieved.

Voted Man of Match / Most Valuable Player. Awarded watch. Int. on Sky / press conf. To reception.

To hotel, then to O'Hagen's for meal. Geech told me playing on Saturday against one James Small. Because of this, came home to look after myself.

Lost/misplaced camera – left in bag in changing rooms.

The weather was atrocious, and running around looking for studs is not the sort of thing you want to do on a match day. But I enjoyed the game. Muddy conditions aren't everybody's cup of tea, but I adapt quite well. Everybody is fast on a dry field, even the props. When it's muddy and heavy it slows a lot of players down. But I can still shift, because I'm quite big in the legs.

I was lucky enough to score with my first touch of the ball as a Lion. It was a coincidence it was a try-scoring opportunity, but it's one to remember.

There had been something else to remember earlier in the day – the moment I was handed my Lions shirt. This little ceremony took place in the team room on match day, in front of the entire squad. Each new Lions player would step forward and be given his shirt by Fran Cotton. I remember taking my shirt and shaking Fran's hand *very* firmly. The lads all give you a round of applause. It's a milestone.

Normally after you've played you go out for a drink, but Geech had tipped me off that I was playing again on Saturday, so I went home to bed.

MATCH REPORT

Border 14 Lions 18

East London, May 28

THE PUNCH-UP between the two Lions hookers in training failed to have the desired effect. Mark Regan and his props, Graham Rowntree and David Young, were outplayed. Fly-half Paul Grayson, carrying an injury, was wayward in his kicking for touch and for goal. It was the rugby league backs, Bentley, Bateman and Tait, who came to the rescue – and tries by Bentley, Regan and Wainwright saved the day. Even so, victory was not secure until Tim Stimpson thumped over a penalty with the last kick of the match.

BORDER – Try: Claasen. Pens: Miller 3.
LIONS – Tries: Bentley, Regan, Wainwright. Pen: Stimpson.

BORDER: R Bennett, K Hilton-Green, G Hechter, K Molotana, A Claasen, G Miller, J Bradbrook, H Hok, R van Zyl (capt), D du Preez, M Swart, S Botha, J Gehring, A Botha, A Fox. Subs: D Maidza (for Molotana 45 min), L Blakeway (Gehring 74), D Coetzer (A Botha 80).

LIONS: T Stimpson, J Bentley, A Bateman, S Gibbs, T Underwood, P Grayson, A Healey, G Rowntree, M Regan, D Young, R Wainwright, G Weir, J Davidson, N Back, E Miller. Subs: A Tait (for Gibbs, 45 mins), M Dawson (Healey 55), P Wallace (Young 68).

'The Lions need more than effort. They need more direction, control, and clear and calm decision-making.'
– *STUART BARNES, Sky TV*

Mud, mud, glorious mud: Scott Gibbs kicks ahead while, inset, John Bentley cuts through the morass at East London

THURSDAY 29 MAY

Selected in team to play Western Province. JAMES SMALL – 55,000. I'll play left wing.

Dave Young still acting the arse.

Lunch – media. Plane (48 seater) from East London to Cape Town. 1 hr 50 min flight in sardine tin nightmare.

Arrived at airport. Usual razz-a-ma-tazz band. To hotel. Usual singers. Interviewed immediately by press ref entertainment. Room mate Eric Miller.

Meal. To British High Commission. Relaxed. Couple of geraniums. Good laugh with all lads. Bed late. Sleep in in morning.

James Small is the biggest name in South African rugby. I had been warned about him back in England by my Newcastle team-mate Inga Tuigamala, who said he was the best player he had ever played against – but very mouthy. He's a passionate player, a little hot-headed at times. People say we're very much alike. It seemed we were destined to meet.

Geech moved me to the left wing so that we would be in each other's faces, which obviously wound Small up. He thought the Lions were making a big thing of it – and he was right. It was our chance to undermine him before the First Test.

Rugby is obviously a team game, but there are individual battles within the team game. I believe that if 10 of the 15 players in your side get over the top of their opposite number, you have a good chance of winning. I go out and attempt to play better than the player opposite me and intimidate him if I need to. I do whatever possible to give myself the edge. If everybody does that in the team you have more chance of success. I knew I had to play well to get a place in the Test team. But I also had to play well to try to undermine Small's confidence.

Now, about those geraniums. Back in Weybridge, David Norrie from the *News of the World* had come and spoken to us about the trappings of being an international sportsman in a foreign country with a high profile. He warned us that if you are sat in a club at two in the morning and this six-foot blonde comes up to you and tells you that you're the best-looking thing she has ever seen, you've got to be a little bit suspicious.

At the High Commission there were two really attractive birds there, but nobody would go near them, thinking it was a set-up. We all jokingly said it could be a plant, so I named them the geraniums. In fact they were probably two very nice girls who wondered why these big beefy rugby players were scared to go near them!

FRIDAY 30 MAY

Sleep in. Not training till 10.30am. Trained. To Newlands Stadium for look/kicking. AWESOME. On top of you – so steep. Kicking was excellent.

Lunch – relax. Lads golf. Nerves building up. Wrote letter home.

INJURIES – Eric Miller relieved, has fractured jaw but can play on. Tom Smith having tests on neck, unknown outcome.

1800hrs team meeting. Meal – relax. Table tennis – Ted.

To bed – nervous. Eric gone out.

Kicking practice with Dave Alred was a real revelation. If you give someone a ball and tell them to kick it, they usually think, well, you just kick the arse off it. But there is a technique. I'm a lot bigger and heavier than Dave Alred, but he can kick the ball a lot further than I can.

It's the way you position your body, the way you hold the ball, the way you place the ball out in front of you, the way you strike the ball, with which part of your foot. The way you keep your head down and your body positioned. And there is a sweet spot on the ball. Goal-kickers like Neil

Doddie's Holiday Snaps

The cake monitor is none other than Bentos the beefcake!

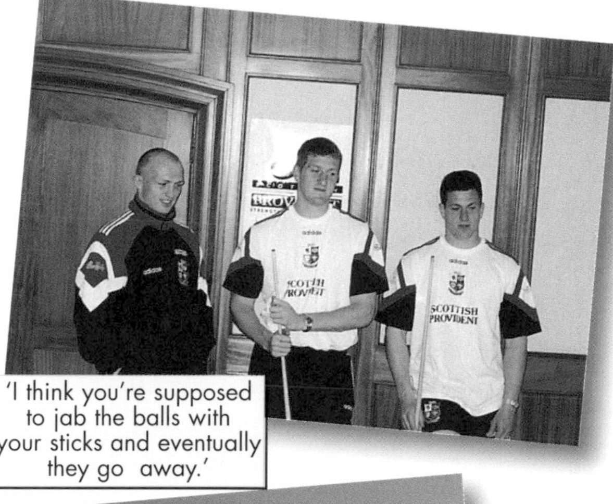

'I think you're supposed to jab the balls with your sticks and eventually they go away.'

'Pull your stomach in Doddie, he's got a camera!' Too late...

'What a biggun.'
'You should see it when it's lit up.'

'You're going to boil me and do what??'

Ieuan's bragging again.

Life on tour. From top: Martin Johnson is greeted by a Zulu band; lineout practice in awesome surroundings; the do's and don'ts of golf by Tony Underwood and Austin Healey

Jenkins and Tim Stimpson practise for hours. I said to Dave: 'Isn't it just like learning to ride a bike – once you learn it you can do it forever.' But it's not. You have to continue to practise.

It's very frustrating at times. I would try to finish a session on a good note, kicking strongly. But then I would come back the next morning and try to go straight into it and kick like an idiot.

It's easy kicking on the training ground, but it's a different kettle of fish going into Ellis Park and kicking in front of 61,000 to win a Test match.

Kicking practice is important for all the backs. There's a hell of a lot of difference between me kicking the ball out on the full and giving them a lineout, or kicking it down the other end of the park and chasing it and putting them under pressure and them kicking it into touch and giving us a lineout. One kick in play can make the difference in a whole game.

SATURDAY 31 MAY

MATCH DAY -v- WESTERN PROVINCE.

Up at 1000hrs. Breakfast 2 x Weetabix.

1100 Team meeting. 3 visits to toilet already. Nerves building up nicely.

12.00 Lunch. Beans on toast. Preparation mentally. Red hot day, no wind – perfect. Pick up shorts & socks.

To ground. Atmosphere picking up.

GAME WON 38-21. Scored 2 tries. Had big battle with Small. Came out on top. He's into sledging big style. Couple of toe-to-toe incidents. He rounded me once on blind side. Had to dig deep. Wouldn't shake hands at end of game claiming that I gouged him. That was to cause him grief later. All lads pleased.

Atmosphere – 51,000 awesome. Had a fantastic enjoyable day. Rang home. Family happy. To hotel.

2000hrs To Cantilla Tequilla. Very

THE JAMES SMALL FILE

The life and fast times of the bad boy of South African rugby

1992 International debut in South Africa's first match after isolation, vs New Zealand (lost 27-24), rapidly followed by a 26-3 humiliation by Australia.
1993 Admits smoking cannabis. Repents in TV ad.
1993 First South African player ever to be sent off (for verbally abusing English referee Ed Morrison in Test against Australia). Opposite number David Campese accuses him of violent play.
1994 First South African player to be cited by the opposition, for a high tackle on Waikato lock Steve Gordon on tour of New Zealand.
1994 Dropped by South Africa after training ground bust-up with coach Ian McIntosh.
1994 Dropped by new South Africa coach Kitch Christie after being seen drinking in early hours.
1994 Involved in a punch-up with a surfer in a bar in Port Elizabeth. Banned from British tour.
1995 Plays throughout triumphant World Cup campaign. Faces Jonah Lomu in final and wins.
1996 Top try scorer (with 14) in Southern Hemisphere's Super 12 club competition.
1997 Accuses John Bentley of eye-gouging in Lions' match against Western Province.
1997 Wins his 38th cap in First Test, equalling the South SAfrican record. Is injured and doesn't play in rest of series.

SMALL ON SOUTH AFRICA v THE LIONS

'I've never forgotten the brilliant 1974 team which whipped us in South Africa. I was five years old, standing on my father's shoulders at the old Ellis Park. To play against the Lions would be the highlight of my career.'

'Carel du Plessis was my hero – the thinking man's rugby player. He could have been South Africa's David Campese.'

'I really like the look of the Welsh guys – Scott Gibbs, Allan Bateman, Scott Quinnell – with that hard rugby league work ethic. They could be key men because it's no picnic touring here. It's relentless, it's very physical and guys like Gibbs need to impose themselves.'

'Jeremy Guscott could be a key factor in the series. If he hits form we could have trouble.'

MATCH REPORT

Western Province 21 Lions 38

Cape Town, May 31

THE TOUGHEST match of the tour so far and by far the best Lions performance. Western Province came into the game with a run of 15 victories and although the Lions' mainly English pack still struggled, the flair of Bentley, Alan Tait and Ieuan Evans brought them a convincing victory backed up by some superb kicking by Tim Stimpson. The Lions started like a steam train with Bentley scoring his usual early try. But then the Province forwards got on top and ground their way to a surprising lead. But with Stimpson out-gunning the Province kickers and Bentley getting under James Small's skin, Rob Howley turned the match with a dazzling break and pass for Evans to score.

WESTERN PROVINCE: – Tries: Muir 2, Brink. Cons: Mongomery 3.

LIONS – Tries: Bentley 2, Tait, Evans. Cons: Stimpson 3. Pens: Stimpson 4.

WESTERN PROVINCE: J Swart, J Small, R Fleck, D Muir (captain), S Berridge, P Mongomery, S Hatley, G Pagel, A Paterson, K Andrews, F van Heerden, H Louw, R Brink, A Aitken, C Krige. Subs: T van der Linde (for Pagel, 56 mins), B Skinstad (Krige, 64).

LIONS: T. Stimpson; I Evans, J Guscott, A Tait, J Bentley, G Townsend, R Howley, G Rowntree, B Williams, J Leonard, M Johnson, S Shaw, L Dallaglio, T Rodber, R Hill. Subs: S Quinnell (Rodber, 63), W Greenwood (Tait, 72).

Scrum-half Rob Howley makes a decisive break. Two weeks later, after showing great form, he went home injured

'This is the third game people have been saying the Lions are vulnerable up front and yet they've won all three. They will cause the Test side a bit of grief.' – *ANDREW AITKEN, Western Province No 8*

'We are here as a squad, and the reason I kicked well was all the help I've had from the other kickers, including Neil Jenkins. I hope that next time Neil is playing he kicks just as well.' – *TIM STIMPSON*

emotional welcome by fans packed into pub/r'ant. Played Oasis Wonderwall which is our adopted tour song. Followed by Simply The Best.

Ted [David Young] and Snake [Scott Gibbs] had big day in hospitality box. Everybody commenting on how I'd 'beaten' Small – Africans and English. Big singsong, boys in good mood. Paul Grayson put up on table as it was his birthday.

Left to rapturous applause, went to Sirens. Drink with Hilda [Richard Hill], Johnno, Lawrence and Ieuan upstairs where had big drink – 1st on tour. Blowjobs [short slammers] and Springboks aplenty. Still riding high on success of game.

0600hrs To bed.

So James Small nearly did me. We both played it very physically: it was a battle within the battle. Throughout the game he was sledging, doubting my playing ability, doubting my parentage: anything to wind me up.

The worst moment – the turning point – came when he went round me in front of the popular stand, caught me flat-footed, kicked the ball forward and they nearly scored. As he ran back past me, he had his finger circling the air, swearing at me and saying: 'I've got you in my pocket.' The supporters in that stand gave me heaps of stick.

I really had to dig deep at that moment, and following that I walled him up. The next chance I got to get to grips with him, I deliberately made my presence felt by tackling him firecely so we both slammed into touch. We had a nose-to-nose altercation, he threw the ball at my head and we had to be split up.

Later, he took a high ball and I was all over him, and he alleged that I had gouged his eye, which I certainly wouldn't have done intentionally. I scored two tries and really he was roasted. He didn't shake hands with me after the game when I offered my hand to him.

The South African press made a massive thing about the way I had psyched him out. He got slaughtered in the press for saying he had allowed himself to be intimidated. Two days afterwards he alleged that I had gouged his eye, which I hadn't. Of course I wasn't allowed to comment on it; Fran Cotton handled that.

I was disappointed that he had resorted to those tactics. I spoke to him after the First Test and told him I was unhappy with some of things he had said and that they were untrue.

Ironically, he was injured in the First Test – the one I didn't play in – so I didn't get to face him in South Africa again.

James Small refuses to shake John Bentley's hand after the match

CHAPTER 7

TOUR DIARY • WEEK 3

When the going gets tough ...

SUNDAY 1 JUNE

UP AT 0830hrs. Boys downstairs. Serious hangover. All boys in bad state. Breakfast – full English. F - - - Dave McClean [the dietician]. Need to soak up beer.

To National Institute for Sport. 45 secs treadmill, 30 secs bike. Had enough. Walk back to hotel, sneak past Fran in reception. Return to bed. Eric arrived back from training 1200.

BAD NEWS. Fran announces that Paul Grayson returning home unfit due to groin injury. Mike Catt sent SOS in Argentina and will replace him. Sorry for him cos he's nice lad.

To airport. 2 hrs flight to Johannesburg. All lads quiet and tired. Press good.

To hotel. Beautiful. Big team room. Room mate – Keith Wood. Legend has it he's a big snorer. Wait & see.

Paul Grayson was the first lad to go home injured from South Africa – but he certainly wouldn't be the last. There were a lot of injuries on the tour.

The worst thing for a player was if he got injured before the Test series even started. That also happened to Doddie Weir, Scott Quinnell and Rob Howley.

Ieuan Evans and Will Greenwood got injured before the Second Test and both went home. Then Keith Wood, Alan Tait and Eric Miller were injured during the Second Test and played no further part in the tour.

Poor old Jason Leonard and Kyran Bracken were injured in the meaningless fixture against Northern Free State between the Second and Third Tests, Gregor Townsend missed the last Test with a hip injury sustained in training, and finally Jerry Guscott and Tony Underwood were both injured in the Third Test.

So 14 players in all had their tour cut short by

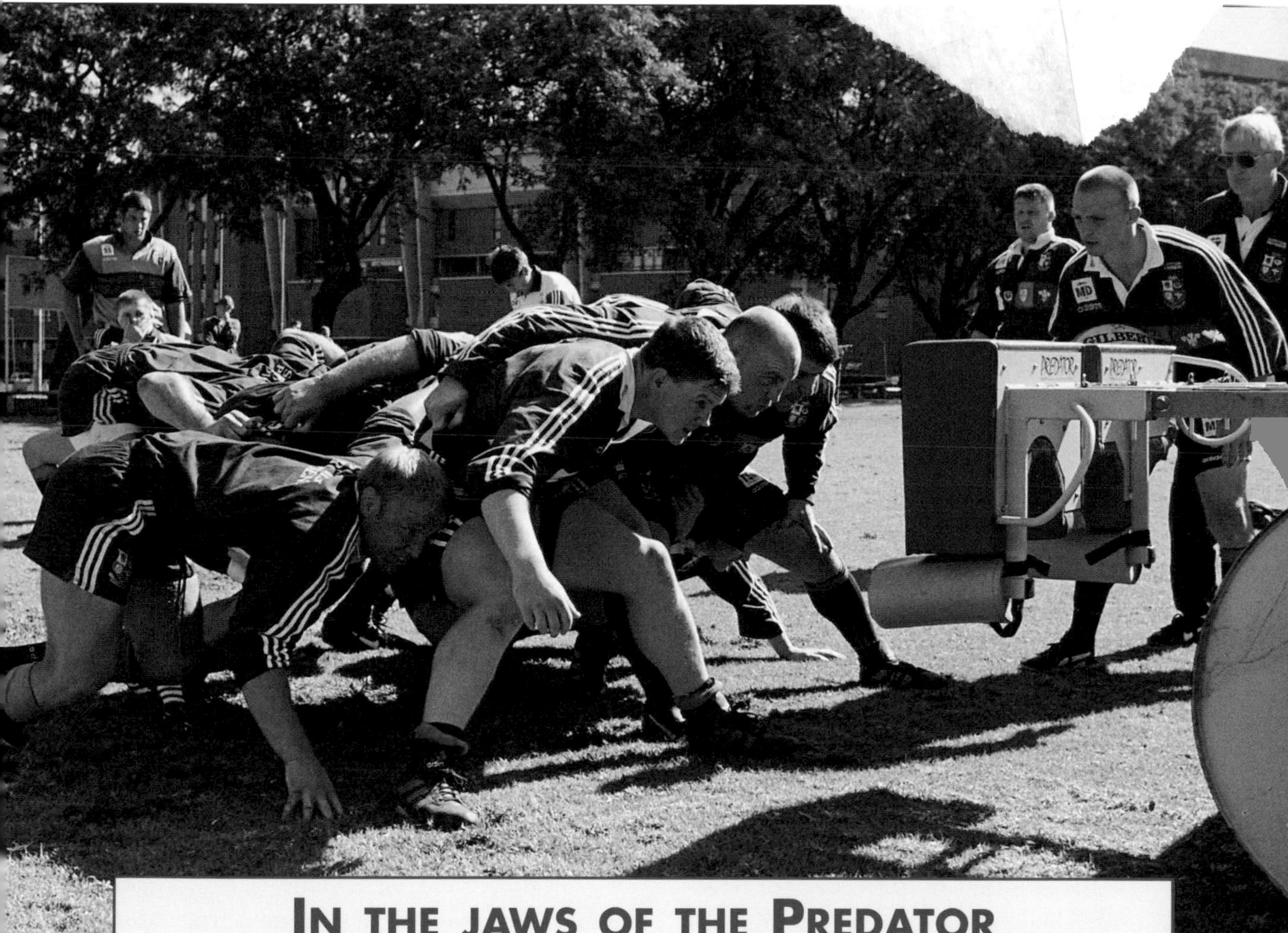

In the Jaws of the Predator

THE FEROCITY of Jim Telfer's scrum training sessions brought tears to the eyes of watchers – let alone those forced to participate. The centre of it all was the Predator scrummaging machine. Devised by former England second row forward Nigel Horton and his company, Richter Engineering, it works by applying pressure forwards and downwards against the opposing front row, and measuring their response. Initially, everyone thought the Test front row would probably be the England trio of Jason Leonard, Mark Regan and Graham Rowntree. They could push 600 kilos against the machine. But the South Africans, it was known, could push 650k. And although the eventual Test front row of Tom Smith, Keith Wood and Paul Wallace could only push 450 kilos, it was decided that since the English power trio would be outmuscled by Os du Randt & co, it was better to opt for the extra mobility of Smith, Wood and Wallace, the Irish prop who only joined the tour when Peter Clohessy was ruled unfit on arrival at Weybridge. Horton explained: 'The decision to go small in the front row was brave but right – it demonstrated the importance of technique in scrummaging.'

injury. We had been warned about it. Dick Best, who had been on the 1993 tour to New Zealand, said: 'Historically, top players always get injured in South Africa. Take two or three out of the Lions' side and they've got problems.'

Finlay Calder, the Scotsman who led the Lions to victory in Australia in 1989, said: 'If the Lions steer clear of injury, I wouldn't be surprised if we win the series. But if we have injuries it will be hard. And no one remembers the teams that lose.'

Paul Grayson had come out on tour still nursing a groin injury sustained way back in March. The Northampton fly-half hadn't played for three months, so there was a question mark over whether he should have been there. When he missed all his goal kicks in the match against Border, Fran said the best place for him was home.

He was replaced by Mike Catt, who a lot of people said should have been on the tour in the first place. Catty was having a sensational tour with England out in Argentina, and with him running the show from fly-half they had just beaten the Pumas in the first Test by 46-20. No wonder Jack Rowell was reluctant to release him to come and join the Lions. In the second Test, without Catt and Nigel Redman – who came out to replace Doddie Weir – England were thrashed 33-13, their heaviest defeat for 50 Tests. But England's loss was our gain.

MONDAY 2 JUNE

James Small accuses me of eye gouging in press. Also saying I bragged about him running past him saying "It was me..... It was me". Total fabrication.

No comment from me. Fran to handle press.

Team selected. I'm rested – pleased.

Hard (very) physical training session. Lunch & relax. Phone call.

Evening to Scottish Prov reception. Girl with legs up to her shoulder blades attraction. Return to hotel.

Me, Barry Williams, Taity, Shawsey to TGI Fridays for drink.

2330 Bed. Forwards have had extremely hard day.

The day that all hell broke out. James Small was all over the South African papers saying that I gouged him. At the lunchtime press conference Fran bit back. 'We are here to talk about rugby,' he said, 'not massage James Small's ego. As far as we are concerned the allegation is nonsense. I suspect the motivation is really to deflect the attention away from the fact that he had a pretty average game and Bentley put two tries past him.'

Small responded: 'It annoys me that people are always prepared to judge my actions without knowing the full story. What he did was not in the rules. He fingered me in the eye when I was defenceless.'

I'll tell you what I told him: that was untrue. The South African management seemed to find it all a bit embarrassing. Coach Carel du Plessis said: 'At this level you have to be able to stay in control and James allowed himself to be weak.' The South African rugby union decided not to cite me – which is what you do when you accuse an opponent of dirty play – so they obviously believed my side of the story.

While all that was going on, I was at the training field watching Jim Telfer give the forwards hell. Their performances to date had undeniably been a bit disappointing, so after the Western Province match Telf decided it was time to get serious. The journalists watching them working out against the Predator scrummaging machine just could not believe it. As one guy said, it seemed like Telf was trying to wear it out. But that's the only way to get results.

TUESDAY 3 JUNE

DAY OFF. Sleep in. Forrest Gump – cried for 1st time since I can remember. Boys golfing. Plan INXS concert tonight.

Laundry needs sorting. Mine & Keith Wood's came back together mixed up. Who knows whose is whose?

To cinema to watch Maximum Risk with boys. To porn shop for videos with Snake (Scottish Prov kitty!!). Meal. Relax.

You're a bit emotional when you're away from home, and I cried in Forrest Gump at the bit where he is introduced to his son for the first time. Later on we saw some silly action film, and then Scott Gibbs and I went out to get a couple of blue movies for the boys.

That was quite funny. I sounded out the lad from Scottish Provident, our sponsors, and said, 'Look, me and a few of the lads want to watch a bit of porn.' He said, 'No problem, give me the receipt.' He probably thought it would just have the price on it. A couple of days later one of the girls from Scottish Provident came up to me and said: 'Bentos, look, how the hell can I present this to my managing director – a receipt for 90 rand for The Love Hut!'

WEDNESDAY 4 JUNE

SADDEST DAY OF MY TOUR SO FAR. DODDIE WEIR'S INJURY.

MATCH DAY. LIONS -v- MPUMALANGA (S.E.TRANSVAAL)

I'm not playing. Keith Wood is – he's ready to ROLL. Sees himself getting stitches today against big nasty pack.

I did speed session with Dave McLean and 6 others. Went well.

Team left hotel at 1215. We left at 1315. Long drive out to Witbank.

John Bentley and Rob Howley can afford to smile – they're not training with the forwards against the Predator machine

MATCH REPORT

MPUMALANGA 14 LIONS 64

Witbank, June 4

IT WAS in this match that Marius Bosman stamped his name in rugby history in the worst possible way. The Mpumalanga lock left his mark on Doddie Weir when he came round the side of a scrum and appeared to kick him deliberately. Weir was left with torn knee ligaments and will play no further part in the tour. Rob Wainwright was lucky not to be badly hurt when Elandre van der Bergh stamped on his face, but at least Wainwright had the satisfaction of a sensational hat-trick scored in eight minutes as the Lions ran riot. A wonderful performance brought them ten tries. The huge Mpumalanga pack were nullified by a Lions scrum with an all Irish and Scots front row, and Neil Jenkins applied the coup de grace with seven conversions and a try.

MPUMALANGA – Tries: Joubert 2.
Cons: Van As 2.
LIONS – Tries: Wainwright 3, Underwood 2, Evans 2, Dawson, Jenkins, Beal.
Cons: Jenkins 7.

MPUMALANGA: E von Gericke, J Visagie, R Potgieter, G Brouwer, P Nel, R van As, D van Zyl, H Swart, H Kemp, A Botha, M Bosman, E van der Bergh, F Rossouw, T Oosthuizen, P Joubert. Subs: A van Rooyen 77 mins for Nel, J Beukes 71 for Oosthuizen.

LIONS: N Beal, I Evans, A Bateman, W Greenwood, A Underwood, N Jenkins, M Dawson, T Smith, K Wood, P Wallace, G Weir, J Davidson, R Wainwright, N Back, T Rodber. Subs: M Regan (for Wood 52 mins), S Shaw (Weir, 56), D Young (Wallace, 74).

Tom Smith digs the ball out of a ruck. After starting as a midweek man, the Scots prop became a Test regular

Team played well.

My tour was saddened today. Doddie Weir – one of my friends and probably the nicest guy on tour – sustained serious knee injury due to his opposite number (Bosman) karate kicking him on knee. Doddie's tour is over.

We travelled back. Big smog around Johannesburg due to all-night fires. Tiring drive back.

Mike Catt has arrived on tour as Grayson's replacement. Seems good lad.

Trained under floodlights. Fast. Glad I'm not a forward. Jim Telfer put them through it on scrummaging machine.

Retun to hotel – meal, physio.

Went to see Doddie. Rob Wainwright there having a whisky with him. Feel like crying. Doddie is such a strong personality, he puts on a brave face. I tell him I could cry and that it's worst day of tour. Doddie never has bad word for anyone.

I come away to write my diary. Spread

A tale of two Scotsmen: hat-trick hero Rob Wainwright dives dramatically to score and, inset, Doddie Weir is injured

'The Bosman incident was a disgraceful act of gratuitous violence that I thought had gone out of international rugby.' – *FRAN COTTON*

'We are more than annoyed with something as cold-blooded as that.' – *IAN McGEECHAN*

'The incidents were unintentional. In one, there were Lions on our side of ruck. And in the other, our lock went for the ball and did not go for the player.' – *GERT GROBBLER, Mpumalanga manager*

photos of Lloyd, Faye & Millie out. I feel lonely for the first time on tour. Listen to Enigma. Don't know where Woody is.

Lessons to be learnt. It could all finish tomorrow. Feel like quitting!! – NO. Must do well – Doddie would want that.

I'll miss him. Good night.

I was very emotional when Doddie Weir had to leave the tour. I nearly cried saying goodbye because Doddie got injured outside of the rules of the game. He got injured by a barbaric act, Marius Bosman karate kicking him in the knee. Doddie's knee ligaments were badly damaged and he feared that he might never play again. It was atrocious.

You can half accept it if you get injured within the rules of the game. It's a physical game. But we are all sportsmen and, no matter what's at stake, you would never put a guy's career on the line.

The South Africans play a very physical way and everything on the floor above grass level got stamped on or kicked. If a lad's got his hand on the ball and he's not supposed to have it, he can expect to have his hand kicked off. Sometimes, when you go on the deck and you can't get out of the way, they give you a right good kicking just for being in the way – even though there's nowhere to go.

People think it must get tougher as you get older, but you also get wiser. It's like the old bull and the young bull. They see a herd of heifers and the young bull says, 'Let's sprint across this field and shag a heifer.' The old bull says, 'No let's walk across and shag them all.' That's so true to life.

The day you start to worry is the day you get injured. There's a fine line between being aggressive but channelling your aggression within the rules of the game, and seeing red mist and going over the top. That's when you become ill-disciplined. One of our strengths was our discipline. It's hard to remain disciplined if you're getting kicked and thumped, nipped and bitten. But it can cost you dear if you start retaliating.

THURSDAY 5 JUNE

Team meeting. Picked to play against N. Transvaal at big stadium. All 4 Newcastle backs selected.

Quiet day. Trained. Getting faster/intense.

Lunch. Doddie in good mood. Interviews with Nick Cain/Steve Bale. Profile on the up.

Relax. Bed early.

Awoke 0500hrs by sperm whale. Pissed. 10 mins story. Spent next 1 hr snoring until I shouted. Claimed he wasn't asleep. Back to sleep.

I called Keith Wood the sperm whale after I filmed him in the swimming pool, submerged up to his top lip and blowing, and he sounded like a whale. He had been playing that day and I hadn't, which is why he was out boozing and I wasn't.

FRIDAY 6 JUNE

Breakfast. Team session in morning.

1445 Me, Lawrence, Rob Howley, Snake went to pictures to see Scream. I had Snake and Lawrence cuddled up to me on either side it was so scary. Their popcorn would fly in the air at the scary bits. Stupid film.

1900hrs Team meeting. Rub [massage]. Relax. Bed 2200hrs.

Red boots from Puma arrived today for me & Snake. Dare I wear them? Not yet!

The only reason I was hesitating about wearing the new boots was because they looked so flash. The days when you had to put vaseline on a pair of new boots and work them in have gone. With the leather they use these days, they are just like slippers. I can get a new pair out of the box on match day and just put them straight on.

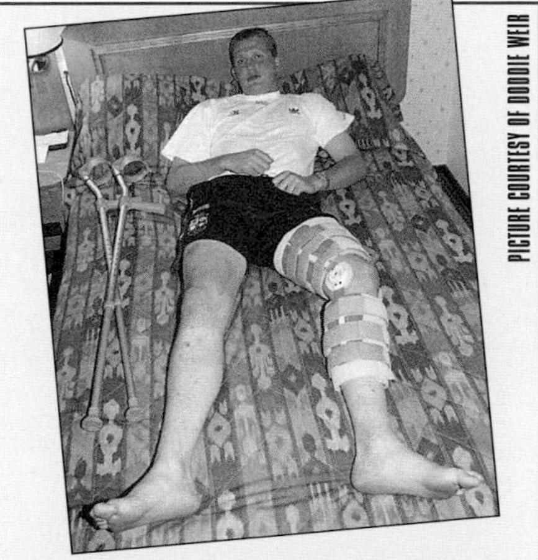

PICTURE COURTESY OF DODDIE WEIR

'At first I thought it was just a knock. I didn't have a clue what had happened or how. Then I realised my knee was very wobbly and thought I had better come off. The odd thing was, there was no pain. If it had happened in a tackle it would not have been so bad – that's a risk you take in rugby. But when I saw the video it made my stomach churn. It was quite deliberate. Bosman deserves all he gets.'
– DODDIE WEIR

Weir called for a life ban on Marius Bosman. In the event, he was simply fined £1,500 and allowed to play on. Doddie recovered much sooner than expected and was able to play in Newcastle's first game of the 1997-98 season.

Doddie limps glumly out of the tour, accompanied by Dr James Robson

MATCH REPORT

NORTHERN TRANSVAAL 35 LIONS 30

Loftus Versfeld, June 7

A SERIOUS setback. After the scintillating victory over Mpumalanga, the Lions came down to earth with a crash. They were behind throughout the match after falling 11-0 behind, and only a flash of Guscott brilliance saved them from a real hiding. England's Triple Crown tight five again failed to make an impression. Gregor Townsend handed Northern Transvaal the spoils when his rash pass to Alan Tait was intercepted by Danie van Schalkwyk. And this against a Blue Bulls side lacking five top players including Joost van der Westhuizen and Ruben Kruger, who were keeping their powder dry in the Springboks camp at Cape Town.

NORTHERN TRANSVAAL – Tries: Van Schalkwyk 2, Steyn, Richter. Cons: Steyn 3. Pens: Steyn 3.

LIONS – Tries: Guscott 2, Townsend. Cons: Stimpson 3, Pens: Stimpson 3.

NORTHERN TRANSVAAL: G Bouwer, W Lourens, J Schutte, D van Schalkwyk, C Steyn, R de Marigny, C Breytenback, L Campher, H Tromp, P Boer, N van der Walt, D Grobbelaar, D Badenhorst, S Bekker, A Richter (captain). Subs: G Esterhuizen (for Lourens, 35 mins), G Laufs (for Grobbelaar, 41 mins), J Brooks (for Tromp, 41), R Shroeder (for van er Walt, 66), A Proudfoot (for Boer, 71).

LIONS: T Stimpson, J Bentley, A Tait, J Guscott, A Underwood, G Towsend, R Howley, G Rowntree, M Regan, J Leonard, M Johnson, S Shaw, L Dallaglio, E Miller, S Quinnell. Subs: S Gibbs (for Bentley, 60 mins), D Young (for Leonard, 75).

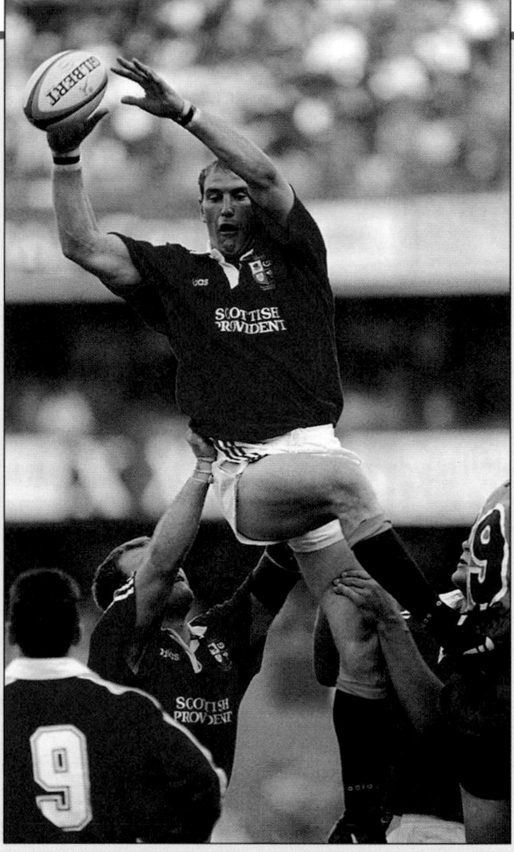

Lawrence Dallaglio towers high above the lineout

'The Lions must realise that if they want to play a Southern Hemisphere type of game they must start scrumming well and driving hard. Scrumming is not just a way of starting the game. Their support play and ball handling are good but are not enough in themselves.'
JOHN WILLIAMS, Northern Transvaal coach

'Mr Gibbs threw a deliberate punch. The explanation of it by Mr Gibbs appears to us to be rather fanciful.' – *JUDGE HENRY DANIELS*

Pretoria High Court judge and head of a three-man tribunal who suspended Scott Gibbs for one match for punching Grant Esterhuizen. Gibbs claimed he had been trying to dislodge the ball from Esterhuizen's arm

SATURDAY 7 JUNE

Match day -v- Transvaal, Loftus Versfeld. Nervous. Also Doddie going home tonight at 2000hrs. Said goodbye now so can concentrate on match. Upsetting.

Roomie – Keith Wood – excellent. Left me alone to concentrate/prepare.

Dai Young gave advice – Keep my head. They'll be watching – he's right. Specially for retaliation following Bosman thing on Doddie. Keep Smiling Be Cool!!! Think of home.

To game, everything feeling OK.

1515 Kick-off (lost 35-30).

Can't believe it. Didn't have a good game. Responsible for first try. Team played poor. Substituted with 20 mins to go by Snake. Very dejected. What a difference a week makes. From top of the world to bottom of the heap.

Quiet remainder of evening at O'Hagen's. Rubbish atmosphere. Sulking. Keep telling myself can't sulk – too selfish.

Decide to go out for an hour. Last-minute decision as bus pulls up outside Speckled Frog as usual. Drink with Lawrence, Carcass, Rob Howley, Snake. To TJ Blondes. Decide to get on it. Blowjobs, the lot. Ed's Diner. Drunk. Saw Wally [Paul Wallace] – Dancing Lawrence legend. Girl wet herself.

0530 Bed.

You have a drink either because you are on top of the world or because you want to drown your sorrows and that was a drowned sorrows night. This was the worst part of the tour for everyone because it was the only defeat, apart from the Third Test. It made us take a hard look at ourselves. We all knew we had to come back strongly in the next match against Gauteng.

Jeremy Guscott dives over the line for one of his two tries at Loftus Versfeld but even he couldn't spare the Lions' blushes

CHAPTER 8

TOUR DIARY • WEEK 4

The Try of the Tour

SUNDAY 8 JUNE

Day off. Scottish Prov golf day for golfers. Meet 0830 in reception. 3 hrs kip. Woody wakes me, dash downstairs. No rush. Breakfast.

To health/rackets club. No Lawrence. Shoot upstairs to wake him. Eventually comes down. Missed bus. Scottish Prov guy David takes us. Get there – Catty coming out, too tired to play. Had coffee since Lawrence said seeing as we're here, we might as well. Return to hotel.

Laze about. Pictures with Robbo, Snake, Ted. Sleep 1730-1900. Meal.

2030 Team meeting. Terrible when you've had a shitter. Not that bad. I will rebound. Must carry on.

Table tennis. Relax. Bed.

At the team meeting, it's embarrassing to sit before all your team mates and watch yourself when you have had a bad game. Watching the match against Transvaal, I was disappointed with myself because I didn't get any opportunites or take any. Sometimes you can get embarrassed big-style in the team meetings. I've experienced that before, but not this time.

No one really did suffer that kind of embarrassment throughout the tour. The coaches were very good, because showing someone up is not necessarily the best way to do it. Nobody makes mistakes on purpose. If you need to speak to an individual, you perhaps should do it privately. Nobody needed that anyway, because everybody played well.

In the match I had been substituted by Scott Gibbs – and, to make matters worse, it emerged that Scott had been cited by the Northern Transvaal officials for punching winger Grant Esterhuizen moments after coming on. Snake was suspended for one match.

Scott Gibbs enjoys an enforced vacation after being suspended for one match for violent play against Northern Transvaal

MONDAY 9 JUNE

Selected for Wednesday's game, which was of no surprise.

Training. Hard session. Contact.

Backy gave Jerry Guscott stitches above eye whilst demonstrating bridge technique.

Lunch. Pictures – Kama Sutra with Doc. Bed.

Scott Quinnell goes home. Sad.

Not yet decided on replacement, probably Tony Diprose.

On tour you don't usually play both Saturday and Wednesday, but I was selected because I had had a bad game. I was expecting it.

The bridge technique, which Neil Back was proudly demonstrating to the rest of the squad, is a tackle technique to secure the ball. Jeremy wasn't too impressed.

TUESDAY 10 JUNE

Free day. Did absolutely nothing all day.

2100hrs Team meeting.

2200hrs Bed.

2300 Switched rooms due to Fester [Keith Wood] snoring. Slept in treatment room.

I spent a lot of time that day thinking. The last game I had played was when we had lost, and I just wanted to be on my own and get my head right. I wasn't sulking but the lads accused me of going off tour a little bit. I had been pretty much the life and soul of things and I suddenly found it hard to continue to do that. Having had a poor game, I felt that I had let people down and I found it difficult to bring the best out of other people. I knew that I shouldn't be like that, but sometimes you just need to forget other people and take care of your own situation. I just hoped that something would happen in the Gauteng match to turn it all around.

MATCH REPORT

Gauteng 14 British Lions 20

Johannesburg, June 11

After the defeat against Northern Transvaal, a win was essential and John Bentley's classic try won it in style. Bentley himself attributed the Lions' success to the forwards, whose hard-driving rolling maul set up Austin Healey's opening try. Mike Catt, newly arrived from Argentina, landed only one kick out of six, but Neil Jenkins came on to secure the vital points that enabled Bentley to win the match.

GAUTENG – Tries: Vos. Pens: Du Toit 3.
BRITISH LIONS – Tries: Healey, Bentley.
Pens: Catt, Jenkins.
Cons: Jenkins 2.

GAUTENG: D Du Toit, J Gillingham, V Veld, H le Roux, P Hendricks, L van Rensberg, J Roux, R Grau (B Swart 65), C Rossouw (J Dalton 52), K van Greuning, B Thorne, J Wiese (capt), A Vos, R Krause, W Brosnihan.

LIONS: N Beal, J Bentley, W Greenwood, J Guscott, T Underwood (N Jenkins 55), M Catt, A Healey, T Smith, B Williams, P Wallace, N Redman, J Davidson, R Wainwright, N Back, T Rodber (capt).

Another match on another continent. Fresh off the plane from Argentina, Mike Catt breaks cover

'There are defining moments on any tour and this is one of them. We defended excellently, attacked decisively and outscrummed Gauteng.'
– FRAN COTTON

'The try was the icing on the cake of a superb team performance. The forwards put in tremendous hard work. We just put the ball over the line.'
– JOHN BENTLEY

'It was the forwards' efforts that got us back into the game. I have never seen such hard work.'
– AUSTIN HEALEY

Tim Rodber, playing the best rugby of his life, runs at the Gauteng defence. In this match the 'Brigadier' was the captain

WEDNESDAY 11 JUNE

Match day -v- Gauteng Lions. Night kick-off 1915hrs. Need big game.

0915 Woke up by Doc wanting to treat Taity. Returned to my room where Fester asleep. Back to bed.

1210 Wake up. Lunch.

1430 Light backs session. Relax.

1915 Kick-off. Beautiful stadium. 40,000 watching. Playing surface not the best in the world. Mediocre first half.

15 minutes to go, leading 10-9. THE TRY. Received ball 5 metres outside my own 22 from a kick which Neil Jenkins caught at full-back. I had got back in support, had looked up to see their hooker, Dalton, stood in front of me. Called for the ball. Set off – went round their No.7 and Dalton into their half. Full-back covering strongly so tried to stand him up but had to go on inside. Then went inside 2 more covering players, at which point found myself on their 22 with posts in front. Head back and went for it. Evaded tap tackle then took 2 players over the line with me. I'd scored!

What a feeling. Suddenly yanked up by half our team and congratulated. Won the game 20-14.

I'm on top of the world. Just what my tour needed at the right time. The elation with which we were greeted upon leaving the field by the non-playing members of the squad and the management was unbelievable. A moment I will never forget. Applauded from field and hugged.

Press conf. Meal with Dr Louis Luyt. 1 hr drive back to hotel and beer in bar.

Bed. Can't sleep. Adrenalin pumping.

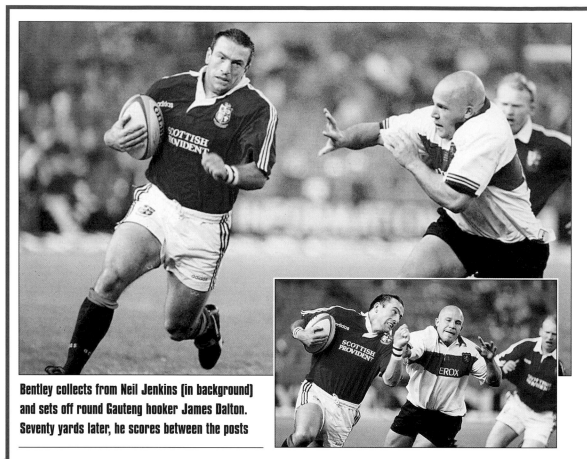

Bentley collects from Neil Jenkins (in background) and sets off round Gauteng hooker James Dalton. Seventy yards later, he scores between the posts

THE TRY OF THE TOUR

Analysed by John Bentley

16 The Sport

Formula One farce leaves Jacques a long way from home

GRAND PRIX

Bentley turbo charge

Cotton cheered by try of tour

RUGBY UNION

IN RUGBY, when the ball is kicked across the field from right to left, people chase after it. It's not an organised chase. People chase hard to where the ball is. The people on the side of the field the ball was kicked *from* don't chase as hard, so there are spaces. I always say that the defending wingers and full-back should try to hit that space.

When that ball was kicked through, Neil Jenkins gathered it and I immediately got behind him because the vision should come from the guy who hasn't got the ball. The guy who's got the ball has to concentrate on collecting the ball and if he gets a clear call from somebody outside him in space, he's got to give him it.

I recall looking up and seeing that they were very disorganised. There was a back-row player and a hooker in front of me with 15 or 20 metres of space outside the hooker to the touchline. I was nearly on our 22. I got the

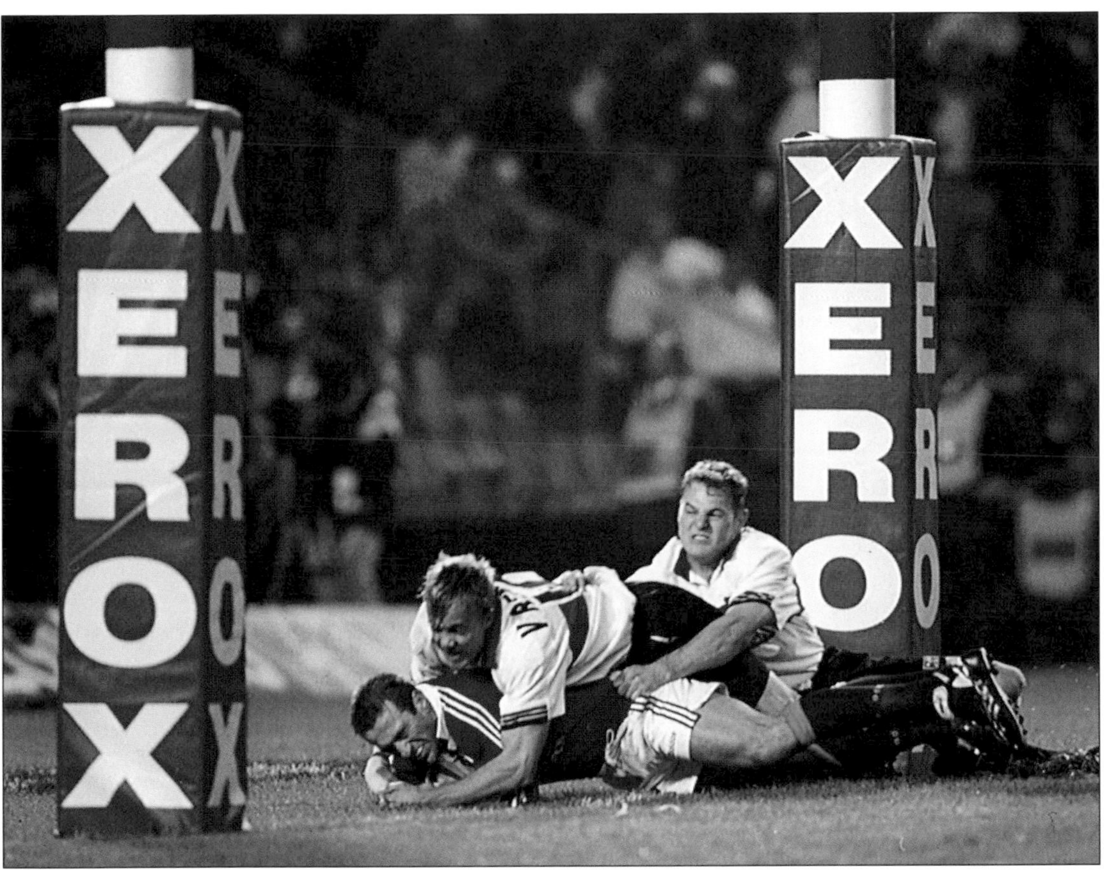

ball and set off and, as I've said before, if I can't get round a hooker, no disrespect to him, I shouldn't be out there.

So I got round those two and the rest of the Gauteng team were covering. I like to run in from the right wing then go back out, because I'm strongest running with the ball in my right arm using a left-hand fend. So I tried to bring the full-back inside, but he was running so fast that he didn't come inside with me, so I had to go inside him completely.

What I tried to do was stand him up. I go inside first to try and make him slow down and check to stop me going inside him – and then I veer back outside, at which point he can't get to me. If I deliberately run towards you instead of trying to run to the corner away from you, that makes you think, bloody hell, he's going to go inside me, so you've got to slow up. You slow down but I'm still going full pace and I swerve out. That's my trademark, but don't tell anyone. Anyway, I couldn't stand the full-back up, so now I was heading for the centre of the field.

Then I saw another player come across and I had to go inside *him* completely. All of a sudden I was on their 22 and the posts were in front of me. And I think it was the back-row lad I had originally gone past who got back and tried to tap tackle me. The guy who had covered across and got flipped on the floor had also got to his feet, and he and the right wing sandwiched me at the same time as I went over the line.

I hate diving and if I can get away with it I don't do it because I don't trust other people not to jump on the middle of my back. But they tackled me as I went over the line. There's a fine line between that and someone coming and dropping on you, which is out of order.

And I had scored. It was quite special really.

After I had scored I remember being hoisted up and greeted by half the team, who were obviously over the moon – Barry Williams and Mike Catt and Neil Jenkins. They were all flabbergasted.

It came at an important time. We had lost on the previous Saturday and the game was balanced at 10-9. It could have gone either way. There were 15 minutes left and as we walked back I remember saying to the lads, 'Let's knuckle down, we can't allow them to get in.'

It was probably the most emotional feeling of my life when the final whistle went. We came off the field and shook hands with their players and obviously there was great elation for the players who had played. But everybody else shared it, too.

At Ellis Park there is a long walk up the tunnel, up a steep staircase to the changing rooms, and every single player who hadn't played and every member of the management, they all formed a tunnel for us. They just did it instinctively, and the elation on their faces and the way we were greeted in the changing room was unbelievable. That just summed up the attitude and the feeling for each other in the squad.

They were so relieved that we had won that game. If we had lost, that would have been two on the trot and we would have been going to Natal a week before the First Test in bad shape. So the tour was back on the road. Frank Cotton said it was a defining moment of the tour.

Immediately after the game I did a live interview with Sky and was then taken to the press conference, so you are pretty much in demand – and then I remember going into a shower and showering alone and thinking, I'm proud of something special here. I didn't really believe what had happened. For the next two days the hype that 'The Try' attracted was phenomenal. All of a sudden, all these people who had been asking 'John Who?' realised why I had been selected.

THURSDAY 12 JUNE

The day after THE TRY. Never been as popular. Try described as ranking among the best ever seen. I'm on Cloud 9.

Trained in morning. Not selected for Natal game.

Travelled from Pretoria to Durban. Still on Cloud 9. Press still talking about try – brilliant – Feet on the ground. Sandy over the moon. WH Smiths – 8 papers full of it.

2300hrs Me, Will, Austin & Wally decide to go out to TJ's for a beer. Ends up being quite a big night. Carcass, Guscott, Stan & Keasty turn up. Excellent night.

Bed 3am. Rooming with Barry Williams.

Mystery player in swimming pool in early hours. It's Will. We'd been warned about Loaded boys who were there. Will to be warned to be careful.

The photographers had warned us that *Loaded* magazine were not coming out to report on the rugby, but to catch the lads on the piss, carrying on with birds – whatever they could get. Next morning there was news flying around that Will Greenwood had been in the pool at 4am...

We were in the foyer waiting to go training, and when Will came out of the lift, the players started to rib him. He pulled me to one side and said, 'What shall I do? Should I tell the management?' I said, 'If they are upset, don't worry, you'll find out about it – you'll be in the office getting a bollocking. Just keep your head down and train hard.'

Later that day Fran summoned him anyway. I went to see Will straight afterwards because he's only a young lad and then I spoke to Fran. He said he hadn't bollocked him, he had just told him to have a bit more nous. Fortunately it didn't reach the ears of the *Loaded* reporter. His feature, when it came out out, was mainly about what a boring lot we were because he hadn't unearthed any scandal.

'Have the Loaded boys gone home yet?' Will Greenwood in training: after a thrilling start, his tour was cut short by injury

FRIDAY 13 JUNE

Still talking about the Try. Brilliant. Press – press – press. Feet on the ground.

1200 To gym with Batman!

Relax in hotel. Do nothing.

You may have noticed by now that I'm very good at doing nothing! I find it keeps me focused and free of stress.

Some observers said it was a shame the players did not see more of the country. Unfortunately that's life in the professional army. We were in South Africa to do a job and, as Fran Cotton said, anyonc who wanted a holiday could stay on at the end of the tour. (Apart from those going to play in Australia, of course!)

SATURDAY 14 JUNE

Sandy's Birthday.

Match day -v- Natal. Not playing.

0915 Training. 10 of us not involved train our bollocks off with Dave McLean & Jim Telfer.

Meet young boy Andrew Wilkins who is brought to hotel by father for "inspirational talk". He met JPR Williams when he was young.

To game. Interviewed on pitch as players warm up before kick-off.

1515 Kick-off. A bit of a bore really. Won 42-12. At a cost.

Row Howley breaks his AC joint on his shoulder. Again, another disappointment

MATCH REPORT

Natal Sharks 12 British Lions 42

Durban, June 14

A stunning victory but at a price. The loss of Welsh scrum-half Robert Howley was a bitter blow a week before the First Test. A dislocated shoulder after just eight minutes spelt the end of Howley's tour. The scoreline reflected the Lions' durability with tries by Gregor Townsend, Mike Catt and Lawrence Dallaglio coming in the last quarter to add to the 24 points from the Howitzer boot of Neil Jenkins.

NATAL SHARKS – Pens: Lawless 4.

BRITISH LIONS – Tries: Townsend, Catt, Dallaglio. Cons: Jenkins 3. Pens: Jenkins 6. DG: Townsend.

NATAL SHARKS: G Lawless, S Payne, J Thompson, P Muller, J Joubert, H Scriba, R du Preez, R Kempson, J Allan, A-H le Roux (J Smit 77), W van Heerden (R Strudwick temp 30), N Wegner, J Slade, W Fyvie, D Kriese.

LIONS: N Jenkins, I Evans, A Bateman, S Gibbs, A Tait, G Townsend, R Howley, T Smith (Leonard 68), K Wood, D Young, M Johnson (Wainwright temp 26), S Shaw, L Dallaglio, R Hill, E Miller.

'I thought it was serious when it happened, but hoped against hope that maybe there was a chance I could just play my way through it. As soon as I tried to throw a pass off my left hand, it was very painful and I knew I was in bad trouble.'

– ROB HOWLEY

'There's a large number of players playing well and they proved the point again today. It's a wonderful position to be in but it makes choosing the Test team terribly difficult.'

– IAN McGEECHAN

Clockwise: Allan Bateman runs; Martin Johnson and John Slade jump; Young, Wood and Smith scrum down; Lawrence Dallaglio flies; Johnson bleeds; Matt Dawson points

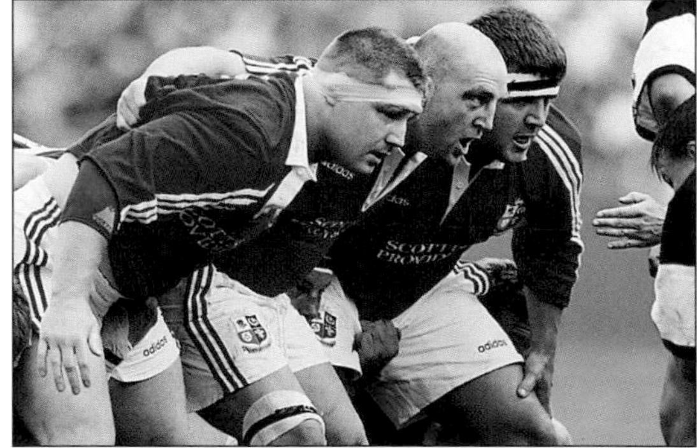

on tour. He has tears in his eyes after in changing rooms. Sad cos his wife/parents & in-laws were all coming out this week. Kyran Bracken to replace him.

After-match function then to hotel.

1930hrs Court session. Judge – Woody. Clerk – Ieuan Evans. Prosecutor – Rob Wainwright. Defence – Ronnie. Enforcers – Shawsy (Bruce), Tom (Randy), Ted (Butch). Excellent. All boys dressed up.

Austin – Gimp – apple/electrical tape, in undies.

Drink can of lager. Management whisky.

Fran Cotton – being boring. Geech/Gregor/replacements – bad time keeping. Telfer – Queen's English.

Jerry Guscott's wife has had third baby girl. Good news.

When Rob Howley got injured it was very sad because his wife, parents and in-laws had all flown out to see him play – and obviously he was a Test certainty. They were talking about him being the star of the tour. It was very hard for him. He was crying in the changing rooms afterwards. It's very emotional at times when you get in the privacy of the changing room. There was a tear in his eye when he went to the hospital because he knew that his tour was over.

The court session was a good way to get people's spirits back up after the shock of losing Rob. And having beaten Natal convincingly that day, everyone was having a good drink.

The court is a touring tradition. It's a fantastic thing for team spirit. It's run very strictly. If you haven't got a bit of dirt on somebody, you'll make something up for everyone else's amusement, and the embarrassment of the individual.

The judge was Keith Wood, the clerk of the court was Ieuan Evans, the prosecutor was Rob Wainwright, the defence attorney was Mark Regan. They were all dressed up in Seventies gear. And then we had three court ushers – Simon Shaw, David Young and Tom Smith – who were dressed up as the Village People with bushy 'tashes and pink vests. Tom was called Randy, Ted was Butch and Simon was Bruce.

What happens is that a player is called to the front. Their first penalty, just for being in court, is to down an alcoholic drink straight away. The lads had to drink a can of lager and the management had to drink a large glass of whisky.

The first accused was Fran Cotton. He was tried and found guilty of being boring.

The next up were Ian McGeechan and Gregor Townsend. They were charged and found guilty for bad time-keeping. Ian McGeechan was always late for meetings, and Gregor Townsend was shocking. I roomed with Gregor twice and he was always late.

The guys who had come out as replacements, like Mike Catt, Tony Diprose and Ollie Redman, they were also convicted of bad time-keeping because they had turned up on tour late, which was quite funny.

Jim Telfer got done for abusing the Queen's English. Because of the passion with which he spoke he used to get his words mixed up and he would eff and blind. He once described Rob Wainwright as being just like a lighthouse in the desert ... f---ing useless.

Austin Healey is a scrum-half. He's a small man and he's got small-man's syndrome, like all small men seem to have. He was annoying to people all the time. You could never get one over on Austin because he always had the last word. They got him out, stripped him down to his underpants, put an apple in his mouth and put black electrical tape all round him, like the gimp in *Pulp Fiction* with the snooker ball in his mouth. And they stuck him in the corner for the whole court session. Everybody was laughing. Except Austin.

Taity's Holiday Snaps

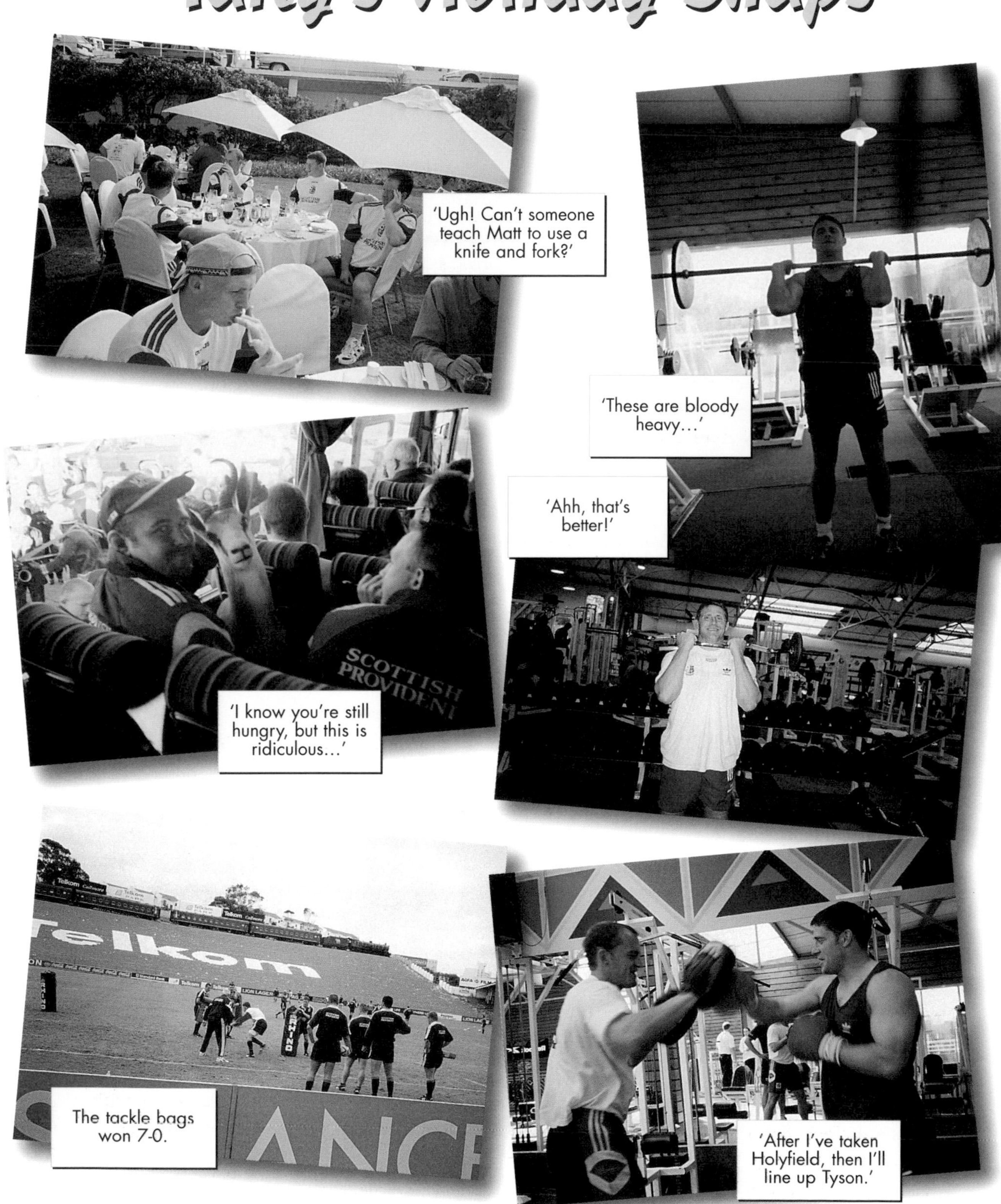

Chapter 9

Tour Diary • Week 5

The envelope under the door

SUNDAY 15 JUNE

Father's Day. Training in morning. Leave Durban for Cape Town.

1730 Arrive in hotel. Rooming with Gregor again. Sort bags out & relax.

1930 Team announced to play Emerging Spingboks. I'm playing. Last game before Test is announced.

Out for meal with Sky TV at restaurant called Blue's. En route bus breaks down – water pump. Blocks road & obstructs 2 fire engines from attending fire. Eventually get there. Good meal – I'm high.

Got training put back 1 hour. Bed 0030hrs.

Because it was a late night I had a word with the management and said it would be good to start training an hour later the next day, which was good for the lads.

MONDAY 16 JUNE

Training. Light team run. Gareth Edwards at training. Introduce myself. My boyhood hero.

Return to hotel where relax.

Dad arrives and phones. Will see him tonight.

Relax. Evening meal. Dad arrives hotel. Hands over parcel from Sandy/kids/Sarah/Mum.

When my dad came out, we were both clear that he was not going to divert me from the tour. When he first suggested it back in England, I turned my nose up a bit but he said, 'Don't worry, I'm not going to be on your heels.' That was one of the

Countdown to the First Test: Back row boys Lawrence Dallaglio, Tim Rodber and Richard Hill; 1974 Lions hero Gareth Edwards visits the training camp; Lions fans hit town; and Rob Howley, a man alone with his thoughts

MATCH REPORT

EMERGING SPRINGBOKS 22 LIONS 51

Wellington, June 17

The battle for Test places reached boiling point as the midweek team turned on the style. Nick Beal, Allan Bateman, Tim Stimpson, Jeremy Davidson and Neil Back all staked a claim with superlative performances in a crushing victory. But it was John Bentley who grabbed the headlines again with a storming 60-yard run to set up the first try of Nick Beal's hat-trick.

EMERGING SPRINGBOKS – Tries: Brosnihan, Goosen, Treu. Cons: Smith, Montgomery. Pens: Smith.

LIONS – Tries: Rowntree, Beal 3, Stimpson, Catt. Cons: Stimpson 6. Pens: Stimpson 3.

EMERGING SPRINGBOKS: M J Smith, D Kayser, P Montgomery, M Hendricks, P Treu, L van Rensburg (Goosen 22), J Adlam (K Myburgh 11), R Kempson (L Campher 68), D Santon (capt), N du Toit, B Els, R Opperman, W Brosnihan, P Smit (K Malotana 65), J Coetzee.

LIONS: T Stimpson, N Beal, A Bateman, W Greenwood, J Bentley, M Catt, A Healey, G Rowntree, M Regan, J Leonard (capt), N Redman, J Davidson, R Wainwright, N Back, A Diprose.

'Bentos played another great game. I was just the lucky one on the end of the moves.' – *NICK BEAL*

'If a crowd gets behind you it certainly helps, and Bentos seems to have brought over a couple of thousand supporters just to cheer him on. He's got his own fan club here now.' – *JASON LEONARD*

Nick Beal gallops clear to score one of his three tries in a sensational performance by the entire Lions team

Tourists in perfect shape to tackle the Springboks after crushing victory

Bentley drives fans wild

Winger's brilliant run spurs on Lions

Replacement poser for Prost

The Emerging Springboks feel the force. Left: Jaco Coetzee runs into Tim Stimpson. Right: McNeil Hendricks tries to swap shirts with Stimpson before the final whistle. Top: Hendricks again – this time he's after John Bentley's boots

reasons why I didn't take the family out. It would have been too much for Sandy to take the three children to South Africa anyway, but I wouldn't have liked to have them there because I would not have been able to remain focused on what I was there for. But it was nice to see my dad.

TUESDAY 17 JUNE

Match day -v- Emerging Springboks. Sleep in to 1030.

1100 Team meet. Mess my trousers. Return to room to change. Light session.

1515 Kick-off. Won 51-22. I have quiet 1st half but good 2nd half.

Sky interview. Inform me that I have been added to England squad. Great news.

Team meeting back at hotel. Test match team will be selected tonight. Told we will find piece of paper under door informing us of details.

Sam Peters, bringer of good news

Treatment. Table tennis/pool with Lawrence. Kyran Bracken arrives.

I am always hyped up on match days, and always have to visit the toilet several times. This was the last game before the First Test and I was so nervous in the team meeting that I actually shit myself, to put it bluntly. But I enjoyed the game.

WEDNESDAY 18 JUNE

BIG DAY. LEARN OF SELECTORS' DECISION REF TEST SELECTION. WE ARE TO HAVE NOTIFICATION OF SELECTION PASSED UNDER OUR DOORS AT 0730HRS.

0530hrs Can't sleep. Await letter. Gregor sleeps like a baby.

Have a shave/bath to pass time.

Waiting outside lift when Sam Peters hands me my letter.

First word – Congratulations. (Over the moon.) Letter reads on to say I am a replacement.

Very disappointed. Feel I've done enough to warrant selection.

Go to breakfast and all lads learn of team. Obviously disappointments.

0930 Team announced. Geech pulls me and tells me it's tactical. I will play a part.

On bus to training at Stellenbosch. Have lunch at wine farm in Stellenbosch. Train in afternoon. Return to hotel.

All lads fall asleep on bus. Everyone tired – long day.

Go out with Carcass in evening for a quiet drink. See Ronnie and Shawsey. Bed.

The way we were informed about Test selection was by receiving an envelope which was pushed under the hotel room door in the early hours of the morning. I went to bed the previous night but I couldn't sleep, waiting to know if I was in the team for the First Test.

I was so uptight I got up at about half-five and had a bath. I was rooming with Gregor Townsend, who didn't seem to share my anxiety.

After a while I went and sat outside the lift in the hotel corridor. I actually video'd myself for the film-makers' documentary, sitting in the corridor. All the lads were fast asleep. At half-past seven Sam Peters came out of the lift with the letters and I scared her to death. So I filmed her posting the letters. I took my letter down to the team room and opened it. I stopped filming then, because of course I didn't get selected. I got picked on the bench. It said 'Congratulations', but it was a massive, massive disappointment and I couldn't bring myself to film the rest of it.

Ieuan was picked on the right wing but surprisingly Alan Tait, who normally plays at centre, was selected on the left wing. Although I had played in that position against James Small and done well, I was on the bench. It was nearly two days before I managed to pick up the camera, I was so disappointed. It was a long, tedious day and to be honest I was a bit fed-up.

Guess who's a Springboks fan and who's for the Lions

THURSDAY 19 JUNE

Training in morning. To Newlands – looks awesome.

1300 Team announced to press. Surprised that I'm not in. Couple of interviews. Relax in afternoon.

1900 Team meeting.

2100 Me, Lawrence, Snake, Leopard, Jeremy Guscott go to Blue's for meal. Good night, good laugh.

2330 Return to hotel. Bed.

The hangover from not being selected. It was a terrible disappointment. You feel as if you've had a leg taken away from you or something, but you can never, never show that. It's very much an inner thing and that's because of the character in the side. If we didn't like each other, you could walk around whining and moaning. But because of the spirit that we had within the squad and because we had identified that it was very much a squad effort, not a 15-man effort, everybody must remain focused.

Obviously I had to handle it very positively, but it wasn't easy.

FRIDAY 20 JUNE

Free day. Relax.

1500 To Kirstenbosch botanical gardens for cup of tea – 21 squad. Waste of time.

Me & Lawrence into Cape Town. Bought eternity ring for Sandy.

Team meeting. Relax.

The day before each Test match, at about 3pm, Ian McGeechan took us out for a cup of tea – the 21 of us, 15 players plus six replacements.

On this occasion it was to a botanical gardens. I wrote in the diary that it was a waste of time because it was a free day and at 3pm it was neither here nor there, it was a bit of an interruption.

A lot of the lads, perhaps myself included, didn't really understand why we were doing this. Geech wanted to get us all together and go out and have a cup of tea and not chat about rugby. It was a pretty strange thing for 21 rugby players to do.

SATURDAY 21 JUNE

Match day. 1st Test.

I'm on bench. Difficult in preparing.

1100 Light breakfast.

1315 Light team run.

1550 To ground.

Atmosphere good.

FIRST TEST

1715 Kick-off. Tense game.
Match won 25-16.
Reception. Undecided on whether to drink or not. Play it by ear.
To hotel. Meal at Cantina Tequila. Me & Carcass stay on. Robert Jones' testimonial. Paul Moriarty/Tony Clement there. Meet Clive Rowlands – nice bloke. Winterbottom/Dooley/Teague/Richards. Hitch a lift on back of flatback lorry. Me & Carcass fight to throw each other off.
Café Sirens. Meet Gavin Hastings.
Very late night. Back to room at hotel with Lawrence.
0715 Pack bags and downstairs. Bed.

I spent the First Test sitting on the bench, and it was sheer torture. It's always easier to play than to watch. Sitting on the bench wears you out more psychologically. The butterflies are shocking. It's emotionally exhausting, knowing that you may be on at any second.

I was so hungry. I got in the changing room at half-time and gobbled a couple of sandwiches and a piece of cake and thought, if I get on now the first thing I will do is throw up all the food I've just rammed down my throat. About 15 minutes from the end I was told to warm up and get stripped, but then the game changed and I didn't get on.

I honestly can't remember much about the match. For most of the time it appeared that we were playing catch-up. We were clawing our way back in with penalties, thanks to their ill-discipline – Neil Jenkins was worth his weight in gold.

And then of course Matt Dawson scored that

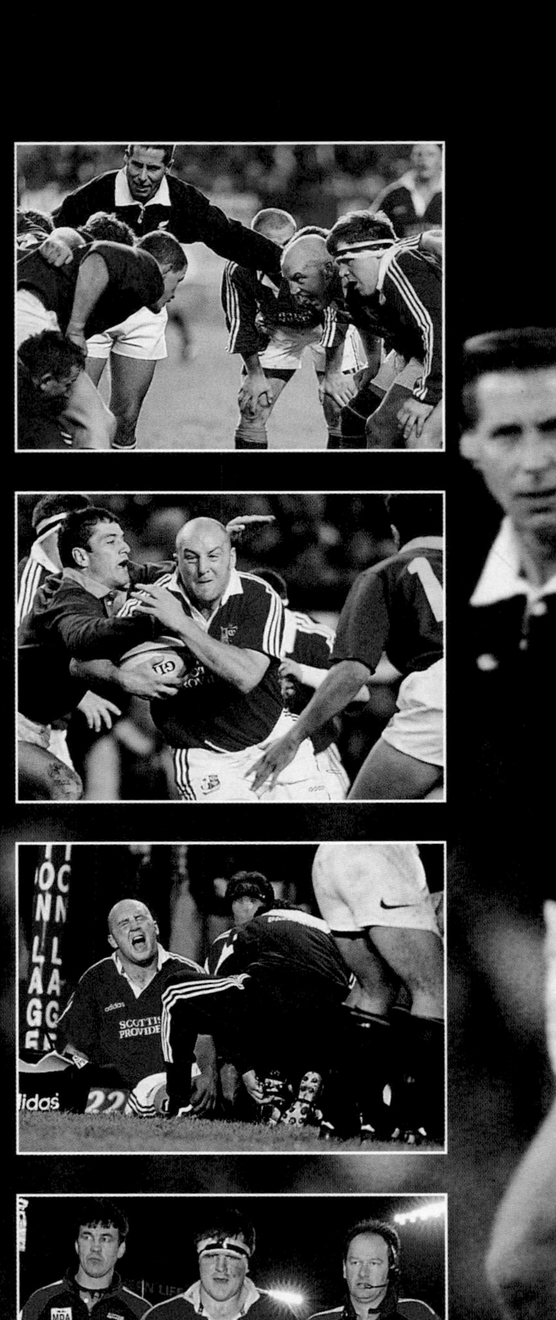

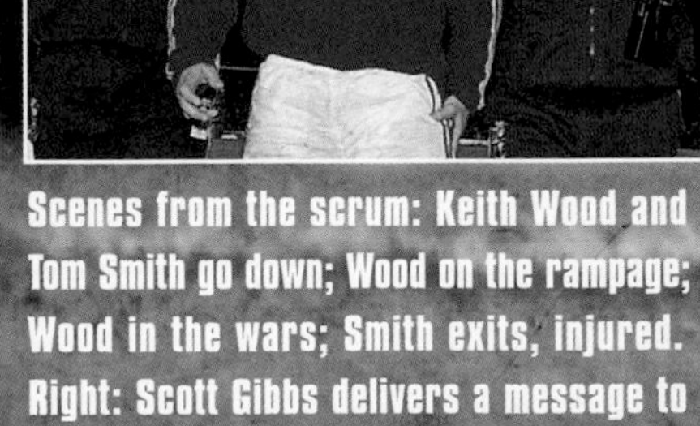

Scenes from the scrum: Keith Wood and Tom Smith go down; Wood on the rampage; Wood in the wars; Smith exits, injured. Right: Scott Gibbs delivers a message to Springboks winger André Snyman

The Sportsunday

PULL OUT

ONLY WITH THE EXPRESS

RAMPANT

BREATHTAKING LIONS STUN SOUTH AFRICA

FULL REPORT AND ANALYSIS: PAGES 2-3

STAY WITH THE SPORT...THE No. 1 PAPER FOR TENNIS

TODAY

Tim Henman tells The Sport exclusively how he can be a

TOMORROW

Our 12-page guide to the world's greatest

SCOTTISH
PROVIDENT

magical try. It was a great moment but it wasn't actually a big surprise because it was a move that had been rehearsed in training. The surprise was that it was Dawse who ended up scoring from it.

The move was called Solo. In it the scrum-half goes on his own down the blind side and he has the option of his winger out on the outside or the No 8 or No 6 who has broken down the blindside with him. But Ieuan had come inside him, so Matt dummied inside to throw it over the top … and everybody stopped and he ended up going over in the corner. It was like slow motion. I don't think he could believe it. And then of course Alan Tait scored an excellent try in the last minute.

We won the First Test, so everyone was celebrating, and yet, because I hadn't played, I was still not sure whether to have a drink. It was nice to have a chat with old warriors like Peter Winterbottom, Wade Dooley, Mike Teague and Dean Richards, and it ended up being a fantastic night. But I was probably there for the wrong reasons.

'The platform was set by the forwards. Because we had control I could get on the outside, around the South African back row and past the blindside defence. They fell for the dummy and I just kept going.'
– MATT DAWSON

'The Lions played very well and took their chances, whereas we had a number of chances and didn't take them. We are going to have a long hard look at ourselves.'
– GARY TEICHMANN, South Africa captain

Clockwise from top left: Matt Dawson saunters in for his try; Lions scorers Alan Tait, Dawson and Neil Jenkins; Ieuan Evans; Tim Stimpson congratulates his fellow full-back; Jenkins the boot; Tim Rodber on the charge

FIRST TEST FACT FILE

CAPE TOWN 21 JUNE 1997

SOUTH AFRICA 16 BRITISH AND IRISH LIONS 25

3 mins Jenkins' kick-off goes straight out. Honiball kicks deep into Lions territory. Lions bring scrum down. Lubbe penalty. **3-0**

6 mins Dawson and Johnson attack. S Africa come in from side of ruck. Jenkins penalty. **3-3**

22 mins South African lineout five yards from Lions line. Andrews wins ball, du Randt powers over. Lubbe misses conversion. **8-3**

33 mins Lions rolling maul brought down. Jenkins penalty. **8-6**

35 mins Evans high kick dropped by Joubert. South Africans dive on ball. Jenkins penalty. **8-9**

HALF-TIME

42 mins Gibbs crash tackles Snyman on halfway. Gibbs attacks, du Randt comes into maul from the side. Jenkins penalty. **8-12**

44 mins After a sustained Springbok attack, Gibbs misses tackle on Teichmann, whose one-handed pass puts substitute Bennett over. Honiball misses conversion. **13-12**

49 mins Wallace comes into maul from the side. Honiball penalty. **16-12**

60 mins Rodber attacks, Kruger offside. Jenkins penalty. **16-15**

73 mins Lions scrum 15 yards from Springboks line. Dawson breaks down blind side, dummies one-handed pass to fool three defenders, and touches down. Jenkins' kick hits post. **16-20**

80 mins Lions move sends ball right across Springbok line for Tait to score in corner. Jenkins misses conversion. **16-25**

What a game. The Lions showed commitment and resilience aplenty, but in the end it was a moment of outrageous impudence that sealed South Africa's fate. Matt Dawson could hardly believe his luck when he made the Tour, let alone the Test team, but he played the game of his life and capped it with an almost comical try eight minutes from the end when he broke down the blind side and fooled the Springbok defence with an outrageous dummy. Alan Tait's last-minute try was the icing on the cake after a defensive performance that was simply superhuman.

SOUTH AFRICA – Tries: Du Randt, Bennett. Pens: Lubbe, Honiball.

LIONS – Tries: Dawson, Tait. Pens: Jenkins 5.

SOUTH AFRICA: A Joubert, J Small, J Mulder, E Lubbe (R Bennett 44), A Snyman, H Honiball, J van der Westhuizen, O du Randt, N Drotske, A Garvey, H Strydom, M Andrews, R Kruger, A Venter, G Teichmann (captain).

BRITISH ISLES: N Jenkins, I Evans, S Gibbs, J Guscott, A Tait, G Townsend, M Dawson, T Smith (J Leonard 75), K Wood, P Wallace, M Johnson (captain), J Davidson, L Dallaglio, R Hill, T Rodber.

Referee: C Hawke (New Zealand).

'This dream started six months ago and it's still going on. That was probably the best fixture I've ever played in.'
– *ALAN TAIT*

CHAPTER 10

TOUR DIARY • WEEK 6

Wounded animal, highly dangerous

SUNDAY 22 JUNE

Train in morning. Had 2hrs sleep.

Train well – professionalism.

Meet Don Rutherford [England director of rugby] who tells me I've been picked in squad to travel to Australia for Test. Brilliant. Ring Sandy – she's pleased. Kids add 7 days on calendar.

1530 Travel to Durban. 2hr flight.

Arrived hotel. Rooming with Mike Catt. Relax.

Back home in Cleckheaton we were in the process of decorating the kitchen and dining area, and the kids had marked up all 56 days of the tour on the wall. Every day they would get their crayons out and cross one off.

Now they would have to add another seven days on to the calendar because I was going to Australia.

MONDAY 23 JUNE

Team for Orange Free State announced. I'm on wing. Need big game to break into Test team.

Training in morning.

1300 Press conference. Announced I'm in England squad.

Free afternoon.

Because we had won the First Test, it was going to be hard to break into the team. And Alan Tait, who had taken 'my' position on the right wing, had scored the try that made the game safe for the Lions. But the management had said we could improve in some areas, so I was very determined.

Tomorrow was going to be the biggest day of my tour so far.

The Lion and the python ... but the deadliest animal in South Africa that week was the wounded Springbok

Will Greenwood's tour comes to a sickening end as he is knocked unconscious in the 40th minute and stretchered off. Top: Greenwood shows his flair earlier in the first half. Opposite: John Bentley scores one of his three tries

MATCH REPORT

Free State 30 British Lions 52

Bloemfontein, June 24

Another brilliant midweek performance was overshadowed by a nasty injury to Leicester centre Will Greenwood, who was knocked unconscious by a crashing tackle from Jaco Coetzee on the stroke of half-time and spent the night in hospital. But the Lions just went from strength to strength, running in seven tries against one of South Africa's top Super 12 sides. The headlines were stolen yet again by that man Bentley with a glorious hat-trick. But there was also an impressive 20-point haul for Free State fly-half and kicker Jannie de Beer, equalling the top individual score against the Lions to date. Hmm...

FREE STATE: Tries: Brink 2, de Beer. Cons: de Beer 3. Pens: de Beer 3.

BRITISH LIONS – Tries: Stimpson, Bentley 3, Bateman, Jenkins, Underwood. Cons: Stimpson 4. Pens: Stimpson 3.

FREE STATE: M Smith, J Van Wyk, H Muller, B Venter, S Brink, J de Beer, S Fourie (H Jacobs 40), D Groenewald, C Marais, W Meyer (D Heymans 60), R Opperman, B Els, C Van Rensburg, J Erasmus, J Coetzee.

LIONS: T Stimpson, J Bentley, A Bateman, W Greenwood (Jenkins 40), T Underwood, M Catt, A Healey, G Rowntree (Leonard 73 temp), B Williams, D Young, N Redman, S Shaw, R Wainwright, N Back, E Miller.

'To me that was one of the all-time great Lions performances, to achieve that, having travelled up here on the day and playing at altitude and against a Super 12 team. I am so proud of them.' – *FRAN COTTON*

TUESDAY 24 JUNE

Match day -v- Orange Free State.

1100 Breakfast.

1215 Party of 30 leave for airport to fly to Bloemfontein.

1600 Arrive at hotel. Light run plus food.

1915 Kick-off. Match goes well. I score hat-trick and get Man of Match. Will Greenwood knocked out and will spend night in hospital.

2230 Leave Bloemfontein airport. Arrive Durban 0030hrs.

Me, Shawsey, Ronnie, Kyran, Catty & Austin to TJ's. Great drink.

Bed 0600hrs.

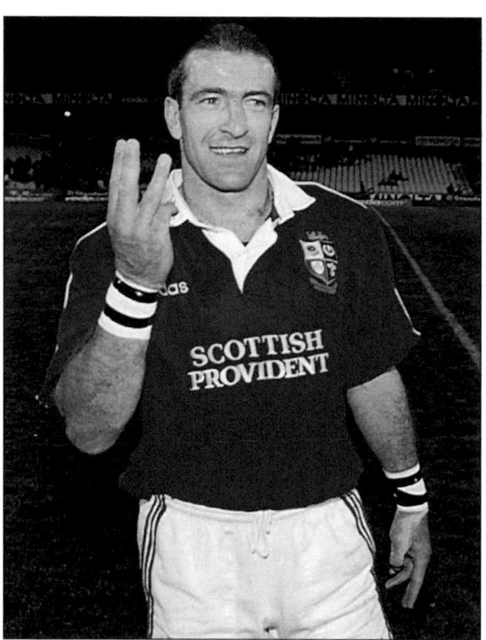

'I was on the end of three tries but it was the forwards who put in the hard work.' – *JOHN BENTLEY*

Basically the South Africans were pissing us about here, because we had to go up to Bloemfontein and play at altitude in between the First and Second Tests.

So rather than all of us go up there, the management decided that anyone who had played in the Test match wouldn't travel with us. The guys who went to Bloemfontein had to make two two-hour plane flights in the day as well as travelling to a hotel in Bloemfontein, arriving three hours before kick-off, and then going on to the match.

It was appalling preparation for the Test match, not only because we had to go up to altitude and play and then come back down, but also because splitting us up like a first team and a second team could have damaged the team spirit. We had a horrible day, even though we won.

Will's injury was pretty nasty. He got concussed, and the doctor said that if it hadn't been for the reaction of the players and medical staff and the facilities available at Free State, he could have died. He was taken to hospital and the doctor decided to stay with him overnight.

But I had a really good game, and was ready to celebrate when we finally got back to Durban. Another very late night! It may seem like we had a lot of them, but they were invariably restricted to match days and perhaps the Thursday for guys who weren't playing on the Saturday.

I know myself. I was training well and the tour was going well for me, so I felt I could afford to do it. It's a way to relax as well. But there were no half-measures. It was very rarely a drink until 11pm and back to the hotel to bed. If we went out, we stayed out.

WEDNESDAY 25 JUNE

1100 match preview. Selectors not prepared to announce team yet. Still to make decisions. Fingers crossed.

1300 Training.

Ieuan Evans tears groin in training. Suddenly it appears I will play. Sad for Ieuan. Wait for news tomorrow morning.

1730 Training. Very tired having travelled/played/drunk last night.

1930 Return to hotel. Too tired to go to Harlem Globetrotters – some of boys go. I have food in Japanese restaurant with Lawrence.

2300 Bed – shattered. Fingers crossed.

Ieuan Evans being injured was obviously not the way I wanted to get into the Test team. When it happened in training, it was very unfortunate for him – and an awkward moment for me.

I didn't want to create the wrong impression by dashing across to sympathise, so I waited until we had a drinks break and just patted him on the back. I didn't speak to him, because it wasn't a good time to talk about it.

I still didn't know if I would be selected. The envelope under the door would arrive tomorrow morning. If I was in, I would find a way to tell Ieuan my feelings about it.

THURSDAY 26 JUNE

0845 Woke up. Letter under door. YES – picked for 2nd Test.

Ring Sandy – she's over the moon.

0930 Team meeting. Team announced.

Training. Photo with 10ft snake on beach front.

1400 Team announced at press conf. Unbelievable. Mass interviews & TV interviews. Father & Sue there. [Sue is my dad's partner.]

1730 Relax in room.

1900 Team meeting.

To Langoustines for meal sponsored by Sky.

2330 Bed.

Schumacher stays ahead in mind games battle

Bentley set to give Lions added bite

Underwood looking for new club

After the team was announced, I went to see Ieuan on my own. There wasn't much I could say. We both knew the situation.

I told him I was sorry his tour had come to an end. I was pleased to be in the team, but it was not the way I would have preferred. I understood how he felt and would try to fill his boots. He said: 'You deserve your chance, so take your opportunity.'

We didn't really need to speak about it. The look on both our faces said it all. An arm round his shoulder would have sufficed.

It was a sad moment, but now I had to put it out of my head and concentrate on preparing for the biggest game of my life.

FRIDAY 27 JUNE

Breakfast. Walk on beach front. Received faxes, which is nice. Hotel is packed with tourists/supporters. Must remain focused.

1145 To King's Park. Dave Alred/ Jenks/Catty punting/kicking. Went well.

1445 21-man squad to bird garden for tea/scones. Bird show. Snake pecked on finger. Good carry-on.

1645 Return to hotel – relax.

Evening meal. Treatment.

When we first went to Durban at the beginning of the tour we had stayed in the most exclusive hotel in South Africa, the Beverly Hills. But now the Boks were in the Beverly Hills and we had been stuck in a beach-front hotel.

To make matters worse, the address of the hotel had been printed in the tour magazine for all the British supporters to read. We all enjoy meeting them, but the night before a Test match it's not ideal. This place was like Butlins – completely crazy.

SATURDAY 28 JUNE

DO NOT BE INTIMIDATED. I HAVE NOTHING TO FEAR. PLAY HARD & WELL. KEEP SMILING.

Match day – 2nd Test.

I'VE RECEIVED MANY FAXES. THERE HAS BEEN A LOT WRITTEN. PRESSURE IS ON. BUT… RELAX & ENJOY.

IT'S TIME TO DELIVER.

THINKING OF EVERYONE AT HOME.

1130 Breakfast. Treatment on troublesome right toe/ankle.

1315 Warm up/back stretch.

Lunch – Beans on toast as usual.

Relax with Catty in room.

1530 Team meeting. Ready to leave…

Although this was the biggest game of my life, I didn't prepare for it any differently to any other game. This is my match-day routine:

I'm not superstitious, but I always do everything the same way. For instance, I strap my ankles in exactly the same way, and I have the left strapped before the right. I strap my left thumb before my right thumb, I strap my ankles before I strap my thumbs. For a little warm-up, I bounce a ball on my chest three times, then I bounce it on my shoulder three times. Always. All of the lads are the same. Some will wear a specific pair of shorts or a special pair of underpants every game they play. Of course they wash them in between…

Your preparation really starts the night before. Obviously you try to go to bed in reasonable time, but not too early. Before all games you tend to be nervous and for big games more so, and you need a good night's sleep rather than playing the game over in your mind and having a restless night. Having had something to eat about 7pm, I would be in my room by about 9pm and then watch some telly and just relax. I usually go to sleep about 11.00.

The night before the Second Test, I was rooming with Mike Catt. He was picked on the bench. I sat on the bench for the First Test and you've got to prepare as if you're playing. It's hard preparing for the bench – it's completely different. If you're getting ready for a 5.30 kick-off you can prepare yourself to explode at that time. On the bench you don't know when you're going to get on.

On the morning of the game I had a light breakfast at 11.30. I usually have Weetabix. On a normal training day you would have breakfast at eight but on a match day you can afford to have a sleep in. Half past eleven may seem late, but we were preparing for a 5.15 kick-off.

I had some treatment on my troublesome right toe and ankle and then I just returned to my room and relaxed. At 1.15 we warmed up. Geech, the coach, got us all together and we lightly went though the moves on a school field, a patch of grass, near the hotel. We had a bit of a stretch and a shake just to get together really.

Every single game I play, about three hours before kick-off I eat four slices of toast with baked beans on them. Beans and bread are beneficial in terms of your performance. Bananas are another thing I eat: I usually have one travelling on the bus to the game. Apart from that I don't eat after three hours before the game because it takes three hours for the beans on toast to digest, and your body uses energy when it is digesting food. Some foods are better than others: steak, pork and salad take a long time to digest whereas a banana takes 20 minutes.

I'm pretty strict with my diet – I wouldn't have a vindaloo curry the night before a game. Most of the other players are the same. For instance, while I'm eating my beans on toast, Neil Back will be eating mashed potatoes, which are also good for energy and digestion. But some of the lads will eat really stupid things like burgers. If you put a steak

Three men awaiting their destiny: Jeremy Guscott, Fran Cotton and Martin Johnson on the eve of the Second Test

in front of them, they'll eat it. You go to a restaurant with them and if there's a free menu, they'll look down the right-hand column where the prices are. That's human nature. The professionalism comes in resisting it.

AFTER LUNCH I relaxed in my room with Catty. In that time I pack my bag, I clean both pairs of boots – I do that religiously every time I play, with polish. I've got my shorts, my socks, my trunks, my gum shield. I've got my toiletries, I've got my blazer and shirt ready to wear after the game.

All Friday night and all Saturday morning I've been trying to relax and think about other things and not get too het up about the game. I've now got two hours just to lounge about and this is when I start thinking about the game. You know there are going to be 50,000 people there and you think to yourself, not a good day to have a bad one with so many people watching!

Because of how the body reacts to nervousness, I have been to the toilet about three times now and my bowels are getting looser. From getting up to kick-off I will usually visit the toilet on four occasions. And I sometimes throw up.

At 15.30 we put our things on the bus and go for a team meeting in the team room. All 47 of us would be there and Fran Cotton will address the squad about the importance of the game. On that particular day he pointed out that we had the opportunity to win the Test series in Durban. Let's take that opportunity. Then he would read out one or two faxes. We had received a fax from Phil Larder and Joe Lydon, the rugby league people, and he said we'd got their respect, they had been impressed by how we played and were wishing us well.

Then Fran would leave the room along with all the lads who weren't playing, and leave Ian McGeechan in the room with the 21 of us.

This was probably the most emotional part of the tour for me because he was a very emotive speaker. I would always sit at the front. When a group of lads go into a room, usually the chairs fill up from the back, but I would always sit at the front and maintain eye contact with him throughout his speeches. A lot of the lads would look down or away, not in disrespect, but in concentration. Just about every time he spoke, because of the emotion inside me and the thought of the family back home, I would get a tear in my eye. He also welled up because he had played for the Lions and coached them on two or three occasions and it meant a lot to him. We all shared that.

It was silent in the room. He's a very quietly-spoken man, not a shouter and banger on the wall. He told us that we had wounded an animal and that's when an animal becomes dangerous. At that moment everybody in that room was prepared to die for each other.

THEN WE would leave the room and get on the bus, where all the other lads were already waiting, and of course they would respect our requirements. They would allow us all to sit together. On the bus I would usually sit in the same seat. When we got to the ground I always wanted to be last off.

Some of the lads talk on the bus but most of us are silent. Travelling to the game was a very emotional time. I would sit in silence and not think about the game but think about all the people at home. I was in charge of the music on the bus and one record I played was from the *Space Jam* film – a song called I Believe I Can Fly. My children had sent me pictures from home saying they believed I could fly, so that was like my song from home. Scott Gibbs noticed that I had tears in my eyes and said: 'It's a special song this, isn't it?'

Imagine travelling to King's Park. There are 52,000 people there and it's choc-a-bloc. We have a police escort and we are driving like thunder.

As you get closer and closer to the ground it becomes harder to remain focused and not notice what is going on outside, because the bus is throwing you around, sirens are going on the police bikes, there's all the British fans cheering and waving. You want to wave and smile at them but you don't. And there are the South African fans, mainly Dutch Afrikaaners. I was impressed that they never stuck two fingers up at us, but they were all jeering and saying: 'You're going to get your arse kicked.'

It's quite intimidating entering King's Park Stadium because when you get off the bus, you have to enter the stadium and walk up the touchline to get to the changing rooms. There was another game going on and although a lot of the crowd were having barbecues in the car park, there were already 20,000 people in their seats and we got a great reception.

Alan Tait straps up his wrists and thumbs in the dressing room. PICTURE COURTESY OF ALAN TAIT

WHEN YOU get in the changing rooms, your shirt is already hanging on your peg. The first thing you do is visit the toilet again. I have my ankle strapped as a precaution – I think prevention is better than cure. I strap my thumbs to prevent them being knocked back. I put my shorts on, then my boots. Then I put a T-shirt on to warm up, stretching in the changing rooms.

At about twenty to five we go out and warm up on the field. I practise kicking and catching the high ball. The atmosphere is warming up, but people aren't paying too much attention to us.

We return to the changing room, where the referee checks our studs. He will have already done the toss-up with Martin Johnson, the captain. There's a quarter of an hour to go before kick-off and this is when, if I'm going to be sick, I'll do it. I bring up all the food I've eaten three hours earlier. Sometimes I get the old fingers down the throat to

A pall of smoke adds to the strangeness as Zulus in tribal dress and Lions fans carrying the Union jack stop the traffic

force myself, just to get shot of it. Of course you're getting plenty of water on board, plenty of liquid.

At this point I always go round and shake the hand of every individual I'm going to play with and wish him all the best – a shake, a hug and a squeeze, saying I hope you have a good game, let's do it today.

Then the hooter goes. We've already come together on a couple of occasions. All 15 of us get round in a circle and link arms. We've done it perhaps six minutes before kick-off and three minutes before kick-off. Then we do it again just before we go out. We're all chipping in with motivational comments, but Johnno has the overriding say.

People all handle themselves in different ways. Some will shout and scream, others are bashing each other about, some are just sat quietly on the bench.

And then it's time to go...

1700 What an atmosphere. We ran out & there was a fantastic cheer. 51,000 there. Gathered in a circle. All of a sudden deafening sound. The place erupted as they ran out.

I always go out third. You run out with real passion. You sprint out and run with the ball and pass it and then the legs go and you feel absolutely exhausted. As we ran out, 10,000 of the Barmy Army on the far terrace gave us a fantastic roar.

We gathered in a circle in our half and then the South Africans ran out and I've never ever heard anything like it. The noise that came from that stadium was absolutely frightening. We were all gathered in a tight circle and I was shouting: 'Listen to that, let's shut this lot up, we don't want this lot on our back all afternoon.' Nobody could hear me.

We're all nervous. It's a fantastic feeling. You're scared of not doing well. The biggest game most of us had ever played in was about to start...

1715 KICK-OFF. Hard game. Didn't play that well. 2 big tackles on opposite number off dock 9 [scrum-half's box kick]. Missed tackle on Joubert who scored.

Final whistle. Won 18-15. Didn't know what to do first. Party time. We went mad. All subs/management/squad on field. Crowd goes crazy.

Sky interviews. Reception.

Return to hotel. Drink in team room. Geech had head shaved No.4 by Woody cos of series win.

2245 Leave hotel. Go with Lawrence, Guscott, Snake, Leopard to meet Barnesy at yuppie café. Steak sandwiches.

0230 To TJ's. Shirt ripped off by Backy/Woody. Big drink.

Take bags downstairs. Bed 0830.

When I won my first cap for England in 1988, I had looked forward to that day all my life. As a seven-year-old I had dreamed of it. For two days before the game I never slept. By the time we kicked off

I was exhausted. I remember the kick-off and the next thing I remember was the whistle for the end of the game. It was finished – and it was such an anticlimax. Nowadays I'm determined to take a step back and enjoy the big games and make an impact. Even so, the Second Test went in a blur.

If rugby players look hyped up at the beginning of a game, it's because you know that within a second of the whistle going, you're going to be running into somebody as fast as you can, getting hold of them and, within the rules of the game, doing anything you possibly can to hurt him. And someone's going to do that to you.

Playing against South Africa I knew that I was going to get a good hiding. You know that you're going to get kicked and bitten, stamped on and gouged. You know that at some point during the game your body is going to be screaming.

We also knew that South Africa would start like a rocket. After the First Test they got slaughtered in the press. As Geech put it in his speech, they were like a wounded animal. We were expecting an onslaught, and we got it. The way they started, I was looking across to our bench to see when they were going to warm the winger up! They got a penalty in the first minute

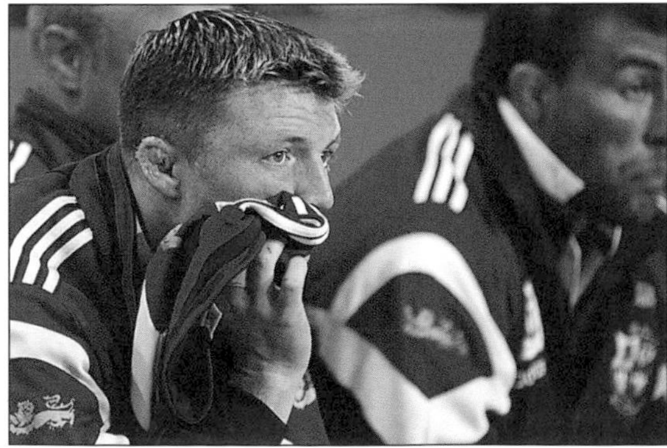

Anxiety on the bench, but Eric Miller can only sit and watch. Opposite: Martin Johnson stalks out with a look that could kill; Matt Dawson harangues the pack. Right: Jeremy Davidson soars above Mark Andrews

SECOND TEST

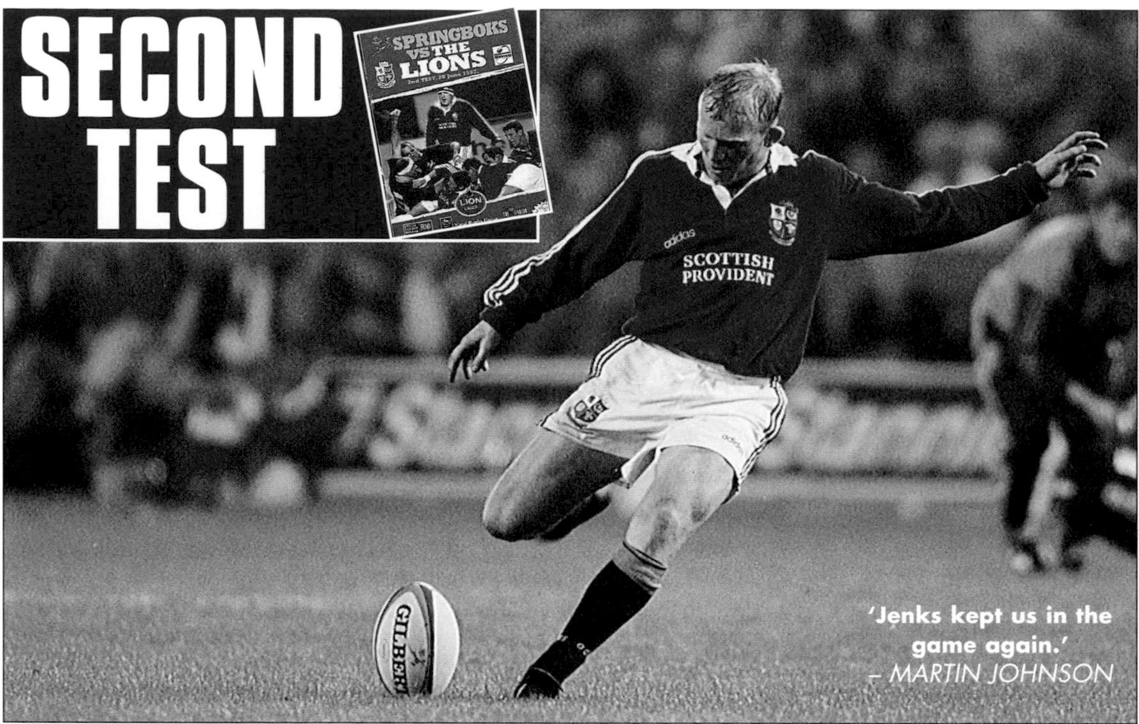

Above: Jenkins the boot punishes South African indiscipline. Below: No way out – Henry Honiball runs into serious trouble. Opposite: John Bentley flattens Pieter Roussow; Gregor Townsend and Joost van der Westhuizen scramble for a loose ball

SECOND TEST FACT FILE DURBAN 28 JUNE 1997

SOUTH AFRICA 16 BRITISH AND IRISH LIONS 25

1 min Springboks' ferocious start catches Lions offside. Honiball misses easy penalty. **0-0**

15 mins Kruger dives on ball in maul near centre circle. Jenkins penalty. **0-3**

29 mins Lions lineout. Springboks collapse rolling maul. Jenkins penalty. **0-6**

34 mins Sustained Springbok pressure. Van der Westhuizen dives through Wood's despairing tackle to score. Montgomery misses conversion. **5-6**

HALF-TIME

40 mins Jenkins drops Honiball's high kick. Tait, under pressure, flicks pass to Honiball who combines with van Schalkwyk to put Montgomery over. Montgomery misses conversion. **10-6**

47 mins Gibbs crashes past du Randt, leaving him KO'd. Davidson takes ball on and is held down in tackle. Jenkins penalty. **10-9**

54 mins Honiball's long pass finds Joubert, who fends off Bentley to score. Joubert misses conversion. **15-9**

65 mins Springboks fail to stay down at scrum. Jenkins penalty. **15-12**

73 mins Lions attack, Teichmann handles on floor. Jenkins penalty. **15-15**

76 mins Townsend drives for line, brought down five yards out. Dawson feeds Guscott, who kicks drop goal. **15-18**

One of the greatest defensive performances of all time enabled the Lions to steal a historic victory and with it the series. The Springboks came at them in wave after wave with tries by Joost van der Westhuizen, Percy Montgomery and André Joubert, but failed to put a single kick between the posts. The Lions clung on thanks to the tenacious tackling of Lawrence Dallaglio, Richard Hill, Tim Rodber and Scott Gibbs. Neil Jenkins, living on scraps, converted all of his five penalties and at 15-15 with six minutes left, Jeremy Guscott wrote his name in Lions history again with an audacious drop goal.

SOUTH AFRICA – Tries: Van der Westhuizen, Montgomery, Joubert.

LIONS – Pens: Jenkins 5. DG: Guscott.

SOUTH AFRICA: A Joubert, A Snyman, P Montgomery, D van Schalkwyk, P Rossouw, H Honiball, J van der Westhuizen, O du Randt, N Drotske, A Garvey, H Strydom, M Andrews, R Kruger, A Ventner, G Teichmann (capt).

BRITISH ISLES: N Jenkins, J Bentley, S Gibbs, J Guscott, A Tait (A Healey 76), G Townsend, M Dawson, T Smith, K Wood, P Wallace, M Johnson (capt), J Davidson, L Dallaglio, R Hill (N Back 57), T Rodber (E Miller 76).

Referee: D Mene (France).

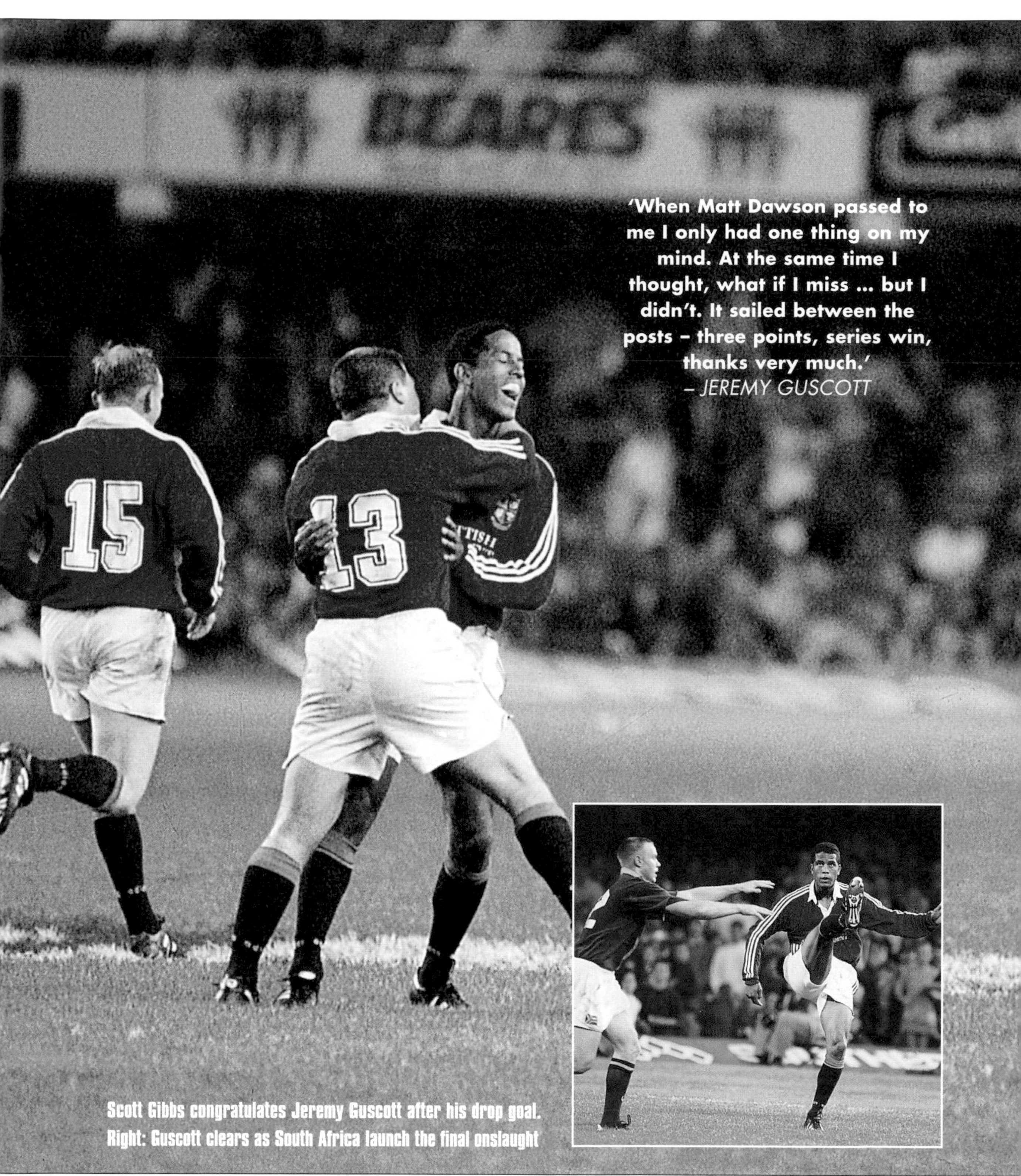

'When Matt Dawson passed to me I only had one thing on my mind. At the same time I thought, what if I miss ... but I didn't. It sailed between the posts – three points, series win, thanks very much.'
– JEREMY GUSCOTT

Scott Gibbs congratulates Jeremy Guscott after his drop goal. Right: Guscott clears as South Africa launch the final onslaught

'A lot of points went begging for the Springboks and Test match rugby is about taking your chances. We took ours 100 per cent and ended up winning.'
– IAN McGEECHAN

but fortunately Honiball missed it. Overall we didn't play well, though our defence was incredible.

I didn't have a great game: I had very little to do, and I missed an important tackle which let André Joubert through to score a try.

But we knew we had a better kicker than they did and in the end that was what counted. They played the best rugby – we kicked the penalties. I can't deny that we were lucky that South Africa didn't pick Jannie de Beer, who kicked so well in the Third Test, but you can go through life looking at what might have been. Yes, he would have been good for kicking the goals. But Henry Honiball is a fantastic fly-half and has been for a long time.

Neil Jenkins by his own admission would not say that he is the best full-back in the world, but his goal-kicking is magic. They used three kickers – Honiball, Montgomery and Joubert – and missed three penalties and three conversions. Jenks took five penalty kicks and landed them all.

But it wasn't a penalty that clinched the series. We were a very fit side and we knew we could play well in the last 20 minutes. We tore some provincial sides apart in the last quarter. That day we hung in there and got stronger, and when the moment came we took it. We worked hard to put ourselves in a position with three minutes left from which we could score – whether by a try, a penalty, or whatever.

And then Jeremy Guscott struck. He did some-

Party time. From far left: Martin Johnson with scorers Guscott & Jenkins; John Bentley; Scott Gibbs and Johnson; Guscott again – or is it Superman?

thing I probably wouldn't have attempted: went for the drop goal. If you miss, you are kicking away possession, so the defending side are often pretty happy to see you try it. But Jerry showed a cool head in the heat of battle, and the feeling when it sailed over was out of this world. I didn't have time to celebrate. My only thought was: Let's get back, there's still five minutes to play ... and I just hope that I don't let them back in!

After that we played on for what seemed an eternity. I've watched it many times since and every time I watch it I think, they've got to score here. Obviously they don't, but bloody hell we were under some pressure. The Boks threw everything at us but somehow we managed to hold out. It was a big last-ditch effort but we had confidence that our team spirit could weather the storm. That went right back to Weybridge.

If the Springboks didn't pick a goal-kicker, it isn't our fault. In 10 years' time, the record book won't say: 'Second Test at King's Park: British Lions 18 – played shocking, South Africa 15 – deserved to win the game'. It will just say 'W' – Test series won, thanks for coming.

We had done what we set out to do way back on May 12. Against all the odds, we had beaten the South Africans on their home turf. We had a big night that night, I can promise you.

Chapter 11

Tour Diary • Week 7

High noon in Johannesburg

SUNDAY 29 JUNE

100hrs Meet for training. Nobody trains. Back to bed. Catty not taken bags down.

1300 Leave hotel. Big farewell. Say goodbye to Ieuan Evans/Will Greenwood.

To airport. Flight 1¼ hr. Sleep. Bus ride to hotel. Sleep. Everyone tired.

1800 Arrive hotel. Cold & like Colditz.

Supposed to be here one-all with all on last match for winner.

2000hrs Bed. Knackered.

Tony Stanger who is on Scotland tour joins us until Friday.

Although I had gone to bed at 8.30, I was down there ready to train at ten o'clock – we all were. But the management said that because we had had a big night we weren't going to train. That was good man-management. A few of the lads went down to the beach, where there were hundreds of fans still celebrating along Durban seafront, but I went back to bed.

New arrival Tony Diprose samples the beach life

We spent the afternoon travelling to a grim industrial town way out in the sticks called Vereeniging. They deliberately took us far away from Durban or Johannesburg to get us away from all the supporters and the razzmatazz so that we could focus on the last Test.

Probably they were expecting us to be one-all in the Test series with all to play for and of course we had bloody won it. Ideally, we should have been in Sun City now for a big last

Robust rucking by Northern Free State, like this moment when lock Koos Heydenrich appeared to stamp on Jason Leonard's head, led to a post-match protest by Fran Cotton. But after seeing the video the Lions manager withdrew his complaint

week, though there would probably have been bother if we had been. But this was really not where we wanted to be.

MONDAY 30 JUNE

0915 Sarah [my sister] rang. Bad news. Grandma died. Can't find Dad to tell him.

Team meet. Not in midweek team. Relieved. Jacuzzi.

Training toned down fortunately. Relax.

Lunch after walk with Woody. Bad smell – abattoir.

1430 Go-karting Grand Prix. Big smash – hurt hip as rammed by Wiggy [Graham Rowntree]. Batman winner. Austin as usual cheats.

1800 Team meet. Bed. Nothing to do here.

There was a shocking smell there. The town smelt of chemicals and the hotel was near an abattoir.

TUESDAY 1 JULY

Match day -v- Northern Free State.

Breakfast. Lounge about. 2 separate coach journeys. Team leave at 1100hrs.

Lunch. We non-players leave at 1300hrs.

1515hrs Match kicks off. Win easily 67-39. TU scores 3.

Travel back after congratulating lads. Chat with Taity. He's off tour. Groin injury. Not bothered. Possibly give TU a run.

Poor old Kyran Bracken had broken off his holiday in the Caribbean after just one day to come out and replace Rob Howley, and didn't get a game until the very last midweek fixture. He scored a try but then injured his shoulder and wasn't able to go to Australia with England.

Alan Tait had played in the first two Test matches and, having won the series, an injury at that stage is easier to take. He knew his absence would probably give his Newcastle team mate Tony Underwood a chance to play – and T.U. was champing at the bit after scoring a hat-trick against Northern Free State.

WEDNESDAY 2 JULY

Morning. What a boring place this is. It is cold & there is nothing to do. It feels as though we lost the series, not won it.

Meeting at 1000hrs. Test side is named today.

Out of 34 players, only 24 fit to train. Woody/Taity/Leopard out of contention with groin/groin/thigh. Jokes about clocking out but nowhere to go.

Still can't find Dad to let him know about Grandma. [He had gone to Victoria Falls.]

Finalise travel details from Sydney to home via Heathrow. Seems ages away – can't wait.

1100 Training. Kicking/lineout.

1300 Lunch. 1530 Training. Didn't go too well. A lot of lads carrying knocks plus tired & fed up. For first time on tour, boys started bickering at each other when things started going wrong.

1830 Signing session at hotel. Shirts dished out & signed.

Evening meal. Some of boys/non-players go out to Sports Café for meal – not me.

Devastation. Realise I've had £400 pinched out of my wallet. Must have gone at same time as Catty had phone pinched. Gutted.

Bed. Letter under door tomorrow revealing Final Test selection.

MATCH REPORT

NORTHERN FREE STATE 39 LIONS 67

Welkom, July 1

Fran Cotton reacted bitterly to the uncompromising rucking of the NFS pack – notably lock Koos Heydenrich, who appeared to stamp on Jason Leonard's head. The controversy overshadowed a free-scoring Lions performance in which Tony Underwood pressed his claim for a Test place with a hat-trick. Ominously, the Lions' tired defensive showing was the worst of the tour.

NORTHERN – Tries: Ehrentraut, Wagener, van Burren, Herbert, pen try.
Pens: Herbert 2. Cons: Herbert 4.
LIONS – Tries: Underwood 3, Shaw 2, Stimpson 2, Back, Bracken, Regan.
Pen: Stimpson. Cons: Stimpson 7.

NORTHERN FREE STATE: M Ehrentraut (J Burrows 68), R Harmse, A van Burren, T de Beer, W Nagal, E Herbert, J Jerling, K Applegryn, O Wagener, B Nell, K Heydrenrich, S Nieuweuhuyzen, H Kershaw, E Delport (A Fouch 74), M Venter.

LIONS: T Stimpson, T Stanger, N Beal, A Bateman, T Underwood, M Catt, K Bracken (A Healey 53), J Leonard (G Rowntree 40), M Regan, D Young, N Redman, S Shaw, R Wainwright, N Back, T Diprose.

'No touring team of our standard should be asked to play with a referee like that or on a pitch that's rock hard. I will be looking very closely at the video because there were some very unsavoury incidents in the game.' – *FRAN COTTON*

There was a lot of thieving going on throughout the tour. The girl who nicked my money probably didn't realise how much she had taken – it may have been a year's wages for her. But for me, losing that cash added insult to injury. We were in a really horrible place, there were so many injuries building up, and everybody was down. It wasn't the best way to prepare for the Third Test.

That morning was my last kicking practice with Dave Alred and Neil Jenkins. I could watch

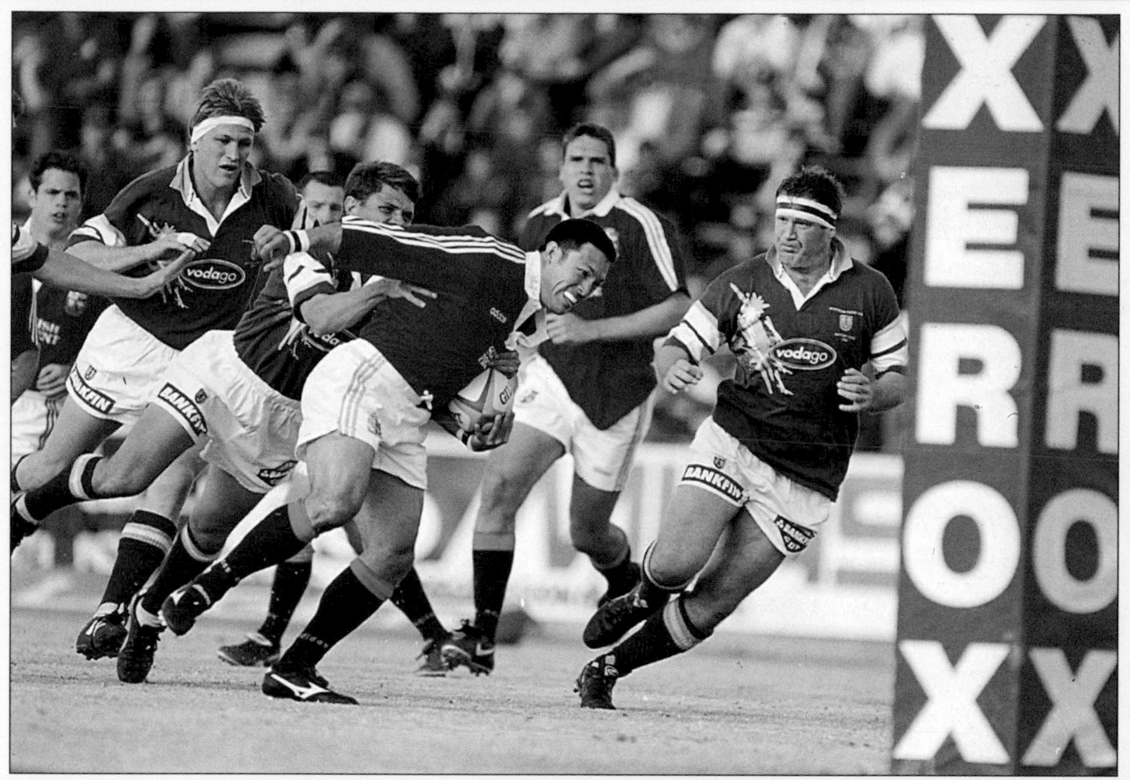

Tony Underwood bursts through to score one of the three tries that made him joint top try-scorer on the tour along with John Bentley. Below: The ups and downs of Kyran Bracken, scoring a try in his only game and then injuring his shoulder

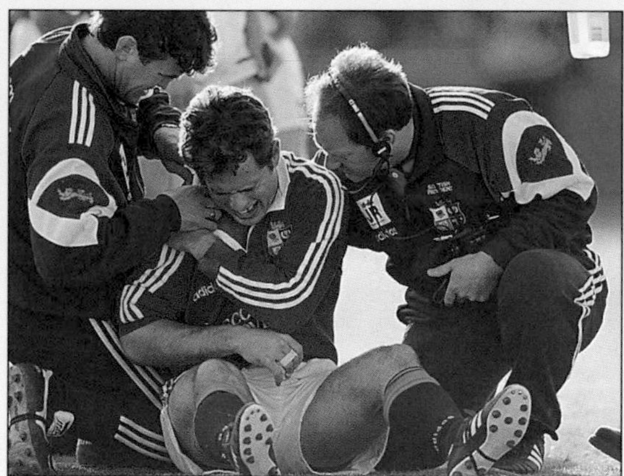

Jenks practise his kicking all day – he is amazing. What people don't see is the amount of effort he puts in. These guys don't just turn out on a Saturday afternoon or a Wednesday evening and kick goals – they spend so much time practising it's admirable. In that inspirational match against Gauteng where I scored The Try, Jenks came on as a substitute after Austin Healey had scored the first try and booted the conversion from the touchline with his first touch. Psychologically that gives you a kick. If you get a penalty anywhere in their half it's three points.

It was obvious the South Africans didn't have a world-class kicker but that was probably down to their arrogance. They thought they would score enough tries not to need the odd bits and bobs. You could say they approached their selection very positively. England over the years have been known to pick full-backs who can't play rugby but can kick goals. Similarly, we went for someone who was possibly not the best full-back on the tour, but as a goal-kicker was second to none.

The South Africans also gave away twice as many penalties as we did. We had done our homework on them. We realised they had bad discipline. By keeping our discipline and punishing their indiscipline by including a world-class kicker, we won a major tactical battle.

That wasn't the only tactical battle we won. We recognised right from the beginning that pound for pound they were stronger men than us. If we tried to physically dominate them we would lose. That's a good admission. That was clever on behalf of the management. So we tried to outfox them.

They were big blokes and strong tacklers. Rather than run directly at them, we would run to the side of them, so they couldn't tackle us with their full body. We knew they played a very physical, aggressive, dominating game where they play head-on and anything in front of them, they just smack it. If you run directly at them, it's food and drink to them, they'll smack you down. So we decided to move them about a bit – a stategy to nullify their back row. Even in the Second and Third Tests, Ian McGeechan felt that they didn't really understand what we were doing.

Dave Alred watches as Tim Stimpson practises the style that made him the tour's top scorer

That was the second big tactical battle we won. Another was the way we set out to run the ball throughout the tour from our own 22.

When the wings and the full-back get the ball back in their own quarter, the tendency normally is to kick it and give away possession. But Geech was saying: 'The players have got to work hard there and get back behind the ball and let's have a go at them.' The way the referees allowed us to hold the ball in the tackle helped us to keep possession, so we were prepared to experiment.

When we are on or near our own line and they are on the attack, that is when their defence is most complacent. They don't expect you to run it. Their winger may drop back expecting the kick, so you've automatically got an overlap. It's just a case of having the confidence to put the ball through hands. We are all strung out in a line, seven of us including the scrum-half, and if their wingers and full-back drop back for a kick, we straight away have a chance to breach their defence. It doesn't come easily to do that, but Geech encouraged that confidence by saying: 'If it's on, it's on.'

Against the provinces we played an expansive game. We weren't able to play the same way in the Tests, because in Test matches the opposition is stronger and you also suffer from nerves. But those provincial matches built up our confidence, not just because we were scoring points but also because of the style we were playing. After being beaten by the Northern Transvaal Blue Bulls we destoyed three Super 12 sides – Natal, Gauteng and Free State. That was very confidence-boosting. And it was a tactical triumph that set up the Test series victory.

THURSDAY 3 JULY

Taity stumbles into room at 0330hrs. Been out celebrating birthday.

0800 Letter under door. Congratulations YOU'RE IN TEAM. Brilliant. I was confident but not over-confident. Never take anything for granted. You always consider downside.

0915 Team announced. 4 new caps. Ronnie, Catty, Back & TU. Stimo & Batman on bench. Pleased for them all.

1000 Training.

1400 Press conf. Pack bags. Nightmare. Always appear to have too much kit.

1700 Leave hotel, travel by coach to Sandton [Johannesburg].

1830 Arrive Sandton. Roomy Catty. Out for meal with Sky.

As you go along the tour you accumulate more and more gear, but you don't get any more bags. We never really unpacked. At each hotel we would split the room down the middle – all my stuff on one side and my room mate's on the other. You would have your laundry done at each hotel, but the rest of your gear stayed in the bags. I hate packing. I just sit there looking at my stuff and expect it to pack itself. I put it off and put it off and end up just shoving it all in any old how, knowing that when I get to the next place I'll regret it.

FRIDAY 4 JULY

0745 Breakfast. Carcass had late night (Gullivers), still in bed. Treatment from Robbo [Dr Robson].

Broke into Carcass's room & pinched his false teeth. Held him to ransom.

Relax all morning. Doddie arrives for last weekend. Great to see him.

1500 Out for customary pre-Test cup of tea at local park. Scones/jam. Good laugh. I took camera.

1700 Haircut with Catty in Sandton shopping centre. Saw Bobby Burrows waiting for someone.

1815 Met Dad at hotel. Told him bad news about Grandma. First time I've ever seen him cry.

1830 Team meeting. Nothing at stake – money/series – but determined to put show on.

2000 Meal. Bed.

Carcass – Mark Davies, the physio – was a legend, an absolutely top man on tour. He hadn't come out with the original tour party, but with Gullivers Sports Travel, so we nicknamed him Gullivers. His two front teeth were false – he was pretty vain and he wouldn't walk around without them. So I broke into his room and nicked them.

SATURDAY 5 JULY

Match day – 3rd Test.

Breakfast. Tim Rodber/Jerry Davidson struggling. Everyone on standby. Rodders pulls out with shits. Rob Wainwright replaces him, Lawrence to blind side.

Photo for YEP [Yorkshire Evening Post] with kids. Pictures, papers, plus good luck messages.

1715 Kick-off. Lost 33-16. Tried hard to play running rugby.

Presentation on field afterwards. Lap of honour. Good atmosphere.

Reception.

2130 To hotel. Change, out to Vertigo's. All sat in circle, big drink.

0800hrs To bed.

I can very rarely say that I play in a game and lose and enjoy it, but that day I did. We played better football in the Third Test than in the other two, even though we didn't win. I got a lot of ball and did a lot of running, and felt I had had an impact.

Although we had already won the series, we still tried hard. That was the last time that a lot of us would ever pull on a Lions shirt and whenever you pull on that shirt you've got to do it justice.

Again South Africa started like a train, but this time the penalty was converted by Jannie de Beer. Within 15 minutes we were 13-0 behind, but then we got into our stride and began putting points on the board. Tony Underwood lifted us with a good run to win a penalty which Jenks put over, but hurt his hip soon afterwards. Then at half-time, with the score 13-9, we lost Jerry Guscott with a broken arm.

The Boks went further away with a scrum-half's try by Joost van der Westhuizen. We might have got back into it when Matt Dawson scored a scrum-half special in reply, but we ran out of gas and they came on strong with tries by Pieter Roussow and André Snyman. And, of course, they kicked their goals. We were all shattered and it's true that we had a lot of injuries in the last week. Keith Wood, Alan Tait and Eric Miller were injured in the Second Test; Jason Leonard and Kyran Bracken were injured against Northern Free State; Gregor

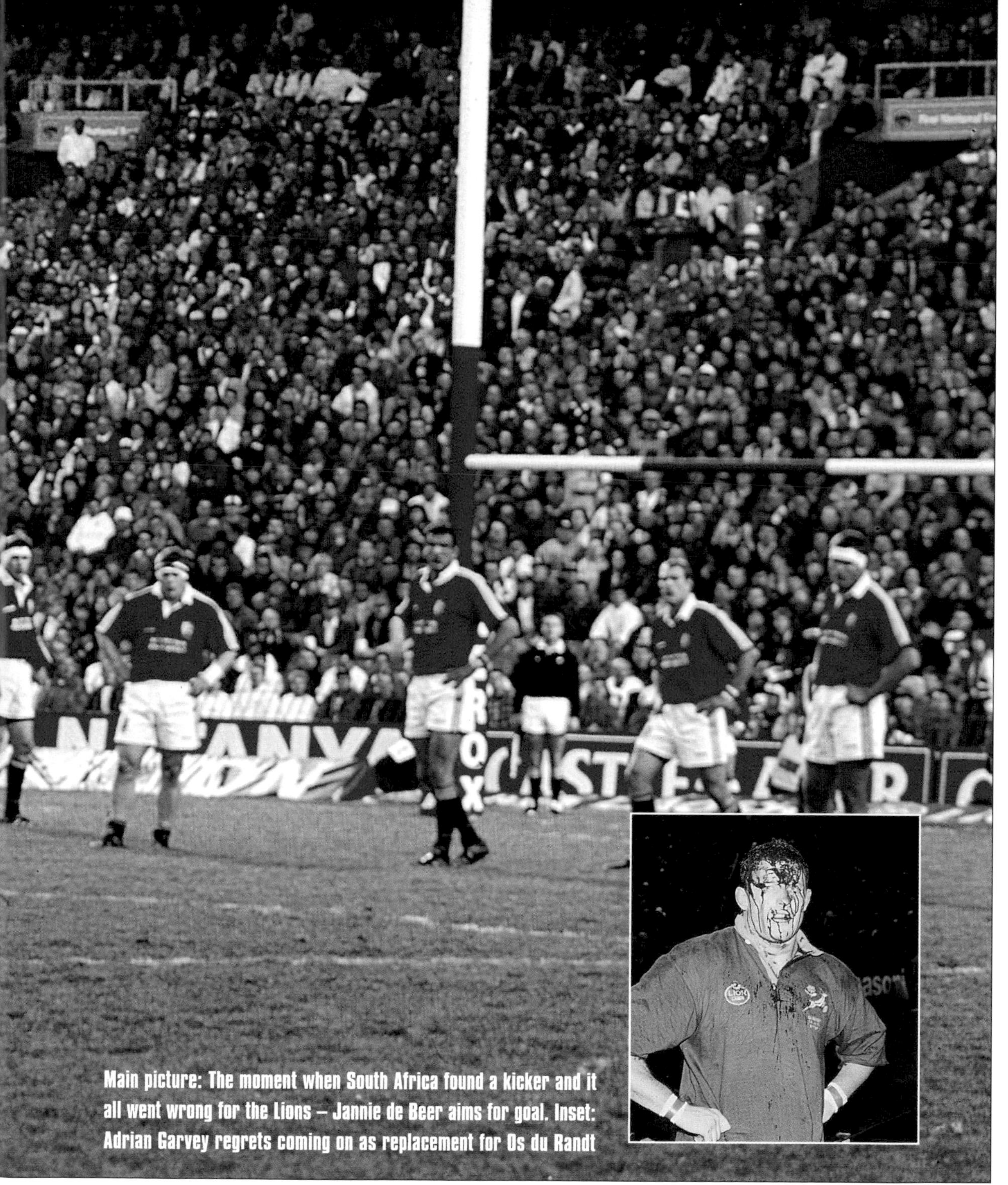

Main picture: The moment when South Africa found a kicker and it all went wrong for the Lions – Jannie de Beer aims for goal. Inset: Adrian Garvey regrets coming on as replacement for Os du Randt

Townsend was injured in training; Tim Rodber fell ill; then Underwood and Guscott were injured. But at the end of the day there are no excuses. South Africa simply played better as the series went on.

At the reception I finally got a chance to speak to some of the guys in their team. I had a good chat with André Joubert and van der Westhuizen. But it's difficult because they've got their wives with them and we're all lads together celebrating – unfortunately, the two don't really mix.

THIRD TEST FACT FILE JOHANNESBURG 5 JULY 1997

SOUTH AFRICA 35 BRITISH AND IRISH LIONS 16

3 mins Dallaglio penalised for coming in at side of ruck. De Beer kicks penalty. **3-0**

9 mins Montgomery stopped by crashing tackle by Guscott, who flicks ball off ground with hand. De Beer penalty. **6-0**

15 mins Repeated Springbok attacks lead to Montgomery try. De Beer converts. **13-0**

19 mins Springboks stray offside. Jenkins penalty. **13-3**

24 mins A series of attacks by Bentley, Dallaglio and Underwood lead to a Jenkins penalty. **13-6**

39 mins Otto fisticuffs with Davidson. Jenkins penalty. **13-9**

HALF-TIME

47 mins After attacks by Roussow and Bennett, van der Westhuizen crashes over. De Beer converts from touchline. **20-9**

60 mins Du Randt on charge, Johnson handles on ground. De Beer penalty. **23-9**

65 mins Lions scrum five yards out. Dawson snipes through. Jenkins converts. **23-16**

74 mins Break by Roussow puts Snyman over. Honiball misses conversion. **28-16**

80 mins Springboks move ball all along line for Roussow to touch down. Honiball converts. **35-16**

The best game of the Test series brought the worst result for the Lions. South Africa finally found a kicker in the shape of Jannie de Beer and the injury-hit Lions were overrun. Yet despite injuries to Jeremy Guscott, who broke his left arm, and Tony Underwood, the Lions persisted with a brave running style of rugby which lit up Ellis Park. Neil Jenkins ended the Test series with a Lions record of 41 points. South Africa regained their pride but Martin Johnson lifted the trophy.

SOUTH AFRICA: R Bennett, A Snyman, P Montgomery (H Honiball 53), D van Schalkwyk, P Rossouw, J de Beer, J van der Westhuizen, O du Randt (A Garvey 63), J Dalton (N Drotske 70), D Theron, H Strydom, K Otto, J Erasmus, A Venter, G Teichmann (capt).

BRITISH ISLES: N Jenkins, J Bentley, S Gibbs, J Guscott (A Bateman 40), T Underwood (T Stimpson 30), M Catt, M Dawson (A Healey 82), T Smith, M Regan, P Wallace, M Johnson (capt), J Davidson, R Wainwright, L Dallaglio, N Back.

Referee: W Erikson (Australia).

Above: A brief shot in the arm for the Lions as Matt Dawson touches down for their only try. Below: The biters bit. The Lions about to get scragged, clockwise from top left, are Scott Gibbs, John Bentley, Jeremy Davidson and Allan Bateman

'We wanted to play some rugby and we did that. In the end it did not quite go our way because our passing tended to let us down.'
– IAN McGEECHAN

'It's been a ten-and-a-half month season for everyone. We are very tired. We tried to dig deep but it wasn't there.'
– MARTIN JOHNSON

SCOTTISH PROVIDENT
adidas
NCP
NATURE'S SOURC

SUNDAY 6 JULY

1400hrs To the outback to Scottish Prov farewell party. Took me 1 hr to drink pint of lager shandy.
Then it all went OFF.
Free bar. Bottles of beer/shooters, press/players, everyone on the piss.

Barry Williams stripped off and taped up due to him getting married next week.

The 'Cup' was filled with champagne and went round. Fran announced tour over. Biggest drink of tour.

Brilliant set of lads. Bar bill £3,000.

We really had a good party because the next day we would be going our separate ways. While the Scots, Welsh and Irish went home, the English boys would carry on to Australia.

That wasn't easy after seven weeks in South Africa. Psychologically we were ready to go home. But playing for your country doesn't come lightly. I was going to Australia to play for England nine years after having last represented them, so it was something I had to do.

MONDAY 7 JULY

Home time. Myself/English boys going to Sydney.

All boys looking forward to my meeting with Jack Rowell.

Took all morning to pack. I hate packing. Stare at it and hope it does itself. Boys returning to England have to have all luggage down to go to Heathrow.

1715 Depart hotel. To Virgin departure lounge. Met Jeff Butterfield in the airport. Nice to eventually catch up with the legend and have a chat about Cleck.

All Krugerrands handed out. Said goodbyes, which are never easy. I have made friends/relationships which will never be forgotten and will remain with me for life.

2030hrs Flight QF24 departs for Sydney. Sit next to Stimo. Flight to Harare, Perth & Sydney – 17hrs total. I have sleeping bomb [pill] after Harare. Sleep all way through. ●

Hands up who wants another party...

LIONS 1997 TOUR STATISTICS

		Played	Sub	Tries	Cons	Pens	DG	Points
Full-backs	Neil Jenkins	6	2	2	17	22	-	110
	Tim Stimpson	6	1	4	23	15	-	111
Wings & Centres	Tony Underwood	7	1	7	-	-	-	35
	Nick Beal	5	-	4	-	-	-	20
	John Bentley	8	-	7	-	-	-	35
	Ieuan Evans	5	-	3	-	-	-	15
	Allan Bateman	6	1	1	-	-	-	5
	Scott Gibbs	5	1	-	-	-	-	-
	Jeremy Guscott	7	-	4	-	-	1	23
	Alan Tait	5	1	2	-	-	-	10
	Will Greenwood	5	1	1	-	-	-	5
	Tony Stanger	1	-	-	-	-	-	-
Half-backs	Paul Grayson	1	-	-	-	-	-	-
	Gregor Townsend	6	-	2	-	-	1	13
	Matt Dawson	4	2	3	-	-	-	15
	Austin Healey	5	2	1	-	-	-	5
	Rob Howley	4	-	-	-	-	-	-
	Mike Catt	5	1	2	-	1	-	13
	Kyran Bracken	1	-	1	-	-	-	5
Forwards	Jason Leonard	5	3	-	-	-	-	-
	David Young	4	2	-	-	-	-	-
	Graham Rowntree	5	1	1	-	-	-	5
	Tom Smith	7	-	-	-	-	-	-
	Paul Wallace	5	1	-	-	-	-	-
	Mark Regan	5	1	1	-	-	-	5
	Keith Wood	5	-	-	-	-	-	-
	Barry Williams	3	1	-	-	-	-	-
	Simon Shaw	6	1	2	-	-	-	10
	Martin Johnson	6	-	-	-	-	-	-
	Jeremy Davidson	7	1	-	-	-	-	-
	Doddie Weir	3	-	1	-	-	-	5
	Richard Hill	5	-	-	-	-	-	-
	Rob Wainwright	7	1	3	-	-	-	15
	Lawrence Dallaglio	7	-	1	-	-	-	5
	Eric Miller	5	-	-	-	-	-	-
	Tim Rodber	5	-	-	-	-	-	-
	Neil Back	7	1	1	-	-	-	5
	Scott Quinnell	2	1	-	-	-	-	-
	Nigel Redman	4	-	-	-	-	-	-
	Tony Diprose	2	-	-	-	-	-	-

Played = Games started. Sub = Appeared as substitute. Cons = Conversions. Pens = Penalty goals. DG = Drop goals.

Taity's Holiday Snaps

Barry Williams would go to any lengths to avoid buying a round of drinks.

'Jason can't hear you, he's got a bottle in his ear.'

One of Martin's stirring pre-match talks.

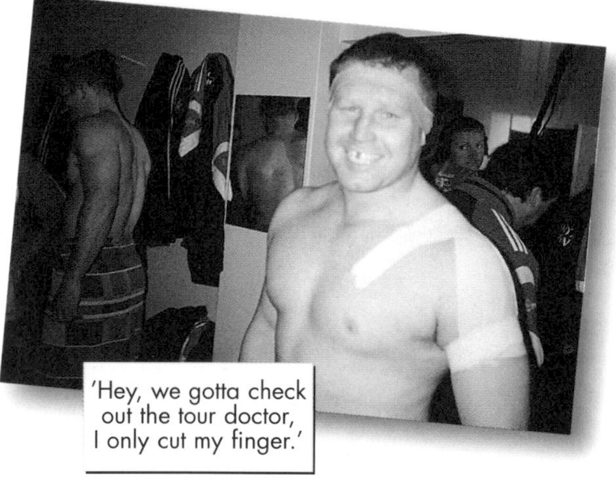

'Hey, we gotta check out the tour doctor, I only cut my finger.'

'Honest, I really can explain everything, please don't take a picture!!!'

'I just drank somebody's what!!'

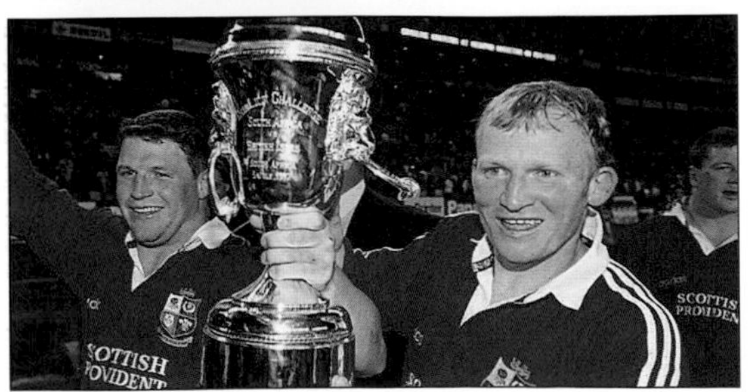

PHOTO CREDITS

All pictures courtesy of Allsport (apart from Doddie and Taity's holiday snaps). **Front cover: Alex Livesey. Back cover: Alex Livesey. Inside flap: Dave Rogers.**

Dave Rogers: 5 (4), 8, 14 (3), 17 (3), 19 (3), 22, 23 (12), 24, 25 (12), 27 (10), 28, 29 (12), 30, 31 (3), 34, 36, 37, 43, 45, 47, 50, 51, 53, 58 (3), 61, 63, 65, 66, 67 (2), 69, 70, 71, 73, 75, 76 (2), 80, 81 (4), 85 (4), 87, 88, 89, 90 (2), 90 (2), 92 (3), 93 (3), 97, 98 (2), 100, 103 (2), 105, 106 (2), 107, 108, 111 (2), 112, 113, 114, 115, 117 (2), 118, 123 (2), 124 (3), 125, 128 (3).

Alex Livesey: 3, 5 (2), 9, 18, 20, 21, 26, 27 (2), 33, 39, 40-41, 43, 55, 58, 60, 74, 77 (2), 79, 80, 81 (2), 86 (3), 95, 98, 99, 103, 107, 108, 109 (2), 112, 113, 117, 123 (2), 124 (2), 128 (2).

Russell Cheyne: 10 (2). Mike Cooper: 19, 59. Howard Boylan: 19. John Etchigi: 15. Clive Mason: 9. Adrian Murrell: 19. Craig Prentis: 9. Allsport: 12 (2), 13, 31, 35, 128.

'That's all, folks!'